YOU GOT THE GIG, HERE'S HOW TO KEEP IT

YOU GOT THE GIG, HERE'S HOW TO KEEP IT

A Working Musician's Model For Success

ANDREW BLAZE THOMAS

Andrew Blaze Thomas

CONTENTS

Dedication		vii
Introduction		1
1	How I Became A Working Musician	5
2	Be Nice	15
3	The Rules Of Time	21
4	Warm Up	32
5	Respect The Gig	36
6	Have Stage Presence	47
7	After The Performance, What's Next?	54
8	Don't Freak Out While Traveling; Airplanes, Tour Busses, and Vans	62
9	Negotiations, What Are You Worth?	72
10	Be Smart With Your Money	78

11	Scheduling Gigs, Paying Taxes, and Child-Support	84
12	Respect Yourself	90
13	How To Handle Getting Fired	100
14	Don't Be The "Jack Of All Trades", Before You Are the Master Of One	106
15	Read Books For Enlightenment	110
16	Avoid Complacency; Always Search For The "Next"	112
17	What Happens When You Lose A Band Member?	115
18	Race And The Blues	119
references		125

Introduction

You Got the Gig, Here's How To Keep It!
A Working Musician's Model for Success
By: Andrew Blaze Thomas

While on tour with my friend, a Blues recording artist, he told me about his struggles to find a steady drummer. "Man, you won't believe this, the last guy I hired got so high before the gig, his eyes were bloodshot red. He couldn't even play the songs right and, to make matters worse, he didn't even care. I tried to instruct him on the gig and he got mad at me. I couldn't believe the nerve of this guy, after the tour, I had to fire him." As my friend relented his frustrations about his ex-drummer, I realized not only was he disappointed, but he was also hurt. If someone asked for a referral for this red-eyed drummer, he wouldn't have anything positive to say. Sometime after I returned from the tour, I ran into the aforementioned drummer at a Blues club in Chicago. He introduced himself during my set break and I knew who he was because his bad reputation preceded him. In fact, if his reputation was great I probably wouldn't have known him by name. The drummer started talking about his drum gear and his current gigs and so on. All I could think was how this guy talks highly of himself when the truth is, he can't keep a gig. After talking with him for a few minutes, I politely let him know that I knew his last employer, and I just finished a tour he was supposed to do with him. At this point he wanted to save face so he downplayed the tour by saying, "The opportunity was small" and, "The tour didn't pay much so it wasn't worth his time." I smiled and nodded without argument because his loss was my gain.

A good reputation is the most important asset in the music business. A musician vouching for you is stronger than any resume, marketing website, social media page, or whatever else you may think that works in your favor. The drummer lost an international touring gig because of his arrogant, condescending attitude which helped create the title of this book. I also received literary inspiration from a separate incident involving one of my friends, who missed out on a great opportunity because of his false sense of entitlement.

My friends dream for his drumming career is like most, play for a major recording artist, earn top dollar, and travel the world playing the biggest of stadiums. With all the practice and chops he consistently works on, he can't seem to find his way. He complains about his church gig he's had most of his life and the bar gigs he still plays to make rent. During our last conversation he told me about a recording session at his church. His church choir was recording a live album and asked him to play drums. They told him they had a small budget and couldn't afford his asking price. He was offended with the counter-offer and said, "NO" to the session. The church hired another drummer and when the record released, it did quite well. My friend was upset because he wanted to be paid handsomely for his work and he suspected the other musicians on the gig were earning more money than him. When he gave his blunt "No" reply to the church, he didn't think he did anything wrong. Bottom line, he didn't see the big picture. After our talk it became clear my friend had a false sense of entitlement, and he didn't understand negotiations which resulted in losing the opportunity to play on a resume building Gospel record. I will illustrate the correct way to handle negations later in Chapter 9.

Some musicians are *in demand* their entire careers, while others struggle to keep a gig. Being in demand is the ultimate success for a working musician, but there is no monolithic path. The music business doesn't come with a manual, so I wrote one. During my career I have made some mistakes and accomplishments that have evolved into life lessons. With over 20 years of experience as a professional drummer, I have established some rules I will share. They are designed to help musicians acquire and maintain a gig. I will share stories from childhood into adulthood that explain how I got into the music business and became one of the most in demand Blues drummers in Chicago. I will also discuss my salary and how it grew throughout my career. The differences in touring salary versus spot date salary and how to negotiate it. The importance of:

    A positive attitude
    Punctuality
    Self-respect
    Image
    Stage presence
    Logging dates in a calendar
    How to:
    Warm up for a gig
    Practice
    Pack luggage for flights
    Travel in vans
    Travel in tour buses
    Handle post show responsibilities
    Network at gigs
    Take advantage of after parties
    Socialize with road and local musicians,
    Accumulate more gigs
    Handle getting fired
    Manage money
    Utilize down-time
    Handle losing a bandmate to being fired or death

I will also discuss why you should pay taxes and child-support, and race; touring as a person of color.

CHAPTER 1

How I Became A Working Musician

I was fortunate to find success in the music business at a very early age. My mother bought me a drum set on my 9th birthday so I could practice in my room after school. She encouraged me to practice because it kept me inside. Living on the west-side of Chicago was dangerous and she just wanted me safe. We attended church every Sunday and I was eager to play drums whenever the Pastors son Thaddeus wasn't around. The gig belonged to Thaddeus and he was a powerhouse drummer. I sat behind him and studied the way he played the bass drum. He played his Slingerland "Speed King" single pedal so fast it sounded like a double pedal. His brothers Danny and Derrick played organ and bass. They were helpful in my early development of playing Gospel music. I played during offering and after church. Whenever Thaddeus missed a service I was there to substitute. After three years of being an understudy, Thaddeus left home for college. In 1990 I was only 12 years old and I had a gig at New Miracle Temple church as the full-time drummer. The church held Tuesday night bible study, Thursday night choir rehearsal, Friday night service, and two services on Sunday. I played all the services for $20 a week. The pay was small and I wasn't a very good drummer yet but I was happy for the opportunity to play. I didn't have plans on become a working musician. I just loved drums and the $20 was icing on the cake. I liked getting paid in singles in a white envelope with my name on it. The singles felt like a big wad of cash in my little suit pockets.

Whenever we had a musical or holiday service Derrick hired the best musicians in town. A few musicians were: Michael Manson (bass player, indie recording artist), Al Willis (guitar player, Isley Bros), and Richard Gibbs (piano, Aretha Franklin) just to name a few. I knew I was a part of something special. I talked with them and listened to their road stories. They talked about how they just flew in from New York or California just in time to make the Sunday morning gig, it all sounded so exciting.

In 1996, I turned 16 years old, and received the opportunity of a lifetime. I played two songs on a live record for our church choir and I got paid $50. Every now and then, I look at that purple cassette tape and I smile. I remember the feeling of hearing myself on a record for the first time. It felt like success! I have been chasing that natural high ever since.

I left New Miracle Temple Church when I enrolled at Western Illinois University. I played in some cover bands but I did not have any musical goals. I never lost my desire to play. However, I did lose my desire to study. I really regret slacking during my college years. After I returned home with a bachelor's degree in 2002, I got a job substitute teaching for Chicago Public Schools. It wasn't music related so I quit within a year. I knew being a school teacher was not my calling.

In 2003, after my short stint teaching, I began looking for opportunities to play music locally. I went to a music store and saw a "drummer wanted" sign on the bulletin board. The band "WHT" was looking for a drummer. I called and set up an audition and discovered it was a metal band. I got the gig after 3 auditions and made friends with the bass player. The metal band barely paid any money. We played for *the door* (music venues either pay by a price negotiated before the show, or by the entrance fee collected at the door; the latter is typical for bands with a small following) and we didn't have much of a following, so I didn't think I would be able to support myself solely as a Rock/Metal musician.

In Chicago, when you play Rock clubs, the business works like this: There are about six bands on most showcases. The door attendant has a clicker counting the attendance. They ask the fans "Who are you coming to see?" The band with the most fans get the lion's share of the money and then it trickles down. To make matters worse, if you perform after the band with the biggest following, they instruct their fans to leave immediately after they perform to attend private parties. Some of these parties start in the parking lot so, you play an empty room while a crowd is right outside and, leave with no money. Chicago Rock clubs are notoriously cheap, some charge a $1 for a cup of water even if you are performing. This is unheard of on the Blues scene.

My friend in the band, Vic Jackson, was a true working Chicago musician and became my mentor. Vic introduced me to musicians at clubs and got me on some auditions. Vic's recommendations afforded me a gig with Chris Greene and New Perspective a Contemporary Jazz band, Gypsi Fari a Reggae band, and St. George a Neo-Soul artist. Also, I was the substitute in a wedding band and some top 40 cover bands. I played in all these bands at the same time. This was all before GPS on phones. There were times I had to call Vic just to get directions to some of the rehearsals and gigs. He took me under his wing and he didn't have to do that. I was just two years out of college and I had already achieved what so many musicians wouldn't. I was working consistently. Things really got serious in 2003 when Vic turned me on to the Blues.

I love to play Blues music because of the sound and its rich connection to African-Americans. Blues music is the soundtrack to the African-American struggle in the United States and Chicago is the home of the Blues. You can listen to live Blues every night in Chicago, which means to a working musician you can earn a livable wage. The Chicago Gospel scene works in parallel with the Blues scene and I can't discuss one without the other.

The Gospel scene is very important to most Blues musicians because it allows us to earn consistent pay and it keeps our chops up. Drummers, bassists, guitarist and horn players earn anywhere from $75 to $350 per week, depending on the size of the church congregation (If you find one paying more, hold on to it!). This also may include a weekly choir rehearsal. Organist can earn $350 and higher per week. Gospel organist make the most money out of all musicians because churches value them the most. Some church Pastors and choirs believe an organist can support a church service musically without any other accompanied instruments. Now that I've discussed Gospel pay, let's get back to Blues earnings.

I really don't think there is any other city in the world where you can earn a living playing only the Blues. Sunday evening you can earn about $100 to $125 plus tips playing Blues bars and clubs in the Chicago-land area. Restaurants pay less on Sundays, about $50 to $100 plus tips. Monday night clubs and bars pay $75 to $125 plus tips. Tuesday through Saturday, bars pay about $100 to $150 plus tips, whereas clubs pay $100 to $250 plus tips. Blues Festivals pay $300-and up, theaters pay $200 and up, and cruises pay $800-1200 per week. New Year Eve gigs pay $200 and up in a bar plus tips and $300-$500 in a club plus tips. In the Blues world, salary is the same amongst side-musicians, whereas in Gospel it depends on what instrument you play.

In 2003, I was offered a gig with Liz Mandville Greeson and the Blue Points. I met Liz at B.L.U.E.S on Halsted after playing at Big Rays Blues Jam. In my opinion, Big Ray's Jam on Wednesday nights was the best Blues open-mic night in the City. Rico McFarland, Chico Banks, Carlos Showers, Roosevelt "Mad Hatter" Purifoy, Carlos Johnson, "BigTime" Sarah, Pookie Sticks, James Knowles, Luke Pytel, Rodney Brown, Jimmy Burns, Bill "the Budda" Dickens, and so many more were regulars in the hosting band. These were some of the most talented Chicago

Blues musicians of the early 21st century. Liz approached me, gave me her business card, and told me she liked my drumming because I didn't play the cymbals a lot. That's how I got the gig with Liz, grooving without bashing the cymbals. She figured I would sound great in her band because she wouldn't have to sing over crashing cymbals. After playing in her band for a few months the word spread that I had a road gig. And then I started getting more gigging opportunities. The opportunities came because I treated the bar gigs as if they were big gigs. I showed up on time and I learned the music. I never charged bands rehearsal fees, and I never drank on stage. In between gigs with Liz I played with Slam Allen who also hired me on the spot after a Big Rays Jam appearance. When I played with Slam Allen it was like a Domino affect. I kept playing open mic night's without bashing cymbals and the gigs came. I had found my niche, playing without bashing cymbals for bands that had singers. Liz's gig was a traditional Blues gig. Slam's gig was more of a party band. I played with Melvin Taylor and the Slack Band, Chainsaw Dupont, and Lindsay Alexander. These were mostly bar gigs that paid anywhere between $50 and $100. I was paying my dues. I rode the city bus and trains all over Chicago to get to rehearsals and gigs. My arms burned as I carried a snare drum, bass pedal, drum stick bag, and cymbals for long walks to bus and train stops. It's tough being a working drummer in Chicago without a car. I asked my family and friends for rides to gigs if I had to bring my whole drum kit. It was a struggle getting rides home after performances because of the late hours. My mother was great in supporting me! I appreciate the nights she drove across the City to pick me up after 2 a.m. I called my friends for rides and I got mad when they came to pick me up with girls in the back seat, blasting music like it's party time. Even though it was tough maintaining several gigs without a car I was feeling some success. I was working constantly, meeting new people but, I wasn't playing internationally. This changed when I met Bernard Allison.

In 2005, Vic and I played Boundary Water Blues Festival in Ely Minnesota with Melvin Taylor and the Slack Band. After our performance, Vic introduced me to Bernard Allison. Bernard is a Blues-Rock artist and son of legendary Blues artist Luther Allison. I saw Bernard's show a year prior and I was excited to learn that he was looking for a drummer. Bernard invited us to sit in his van and listen to some demo tracks of his new album "Higher Power." I was impressed by how well the band sounded. During our listening session, Vic gave Bernard a CD of Chris Greene's latest album "Jazz," which we both played on. I was nervous when I realized my Chris Greene record would serve as an auditioning tool. Vic had set it up that way and I am glad he did because Bernard liked the CD and hired me on the spot. About a month later, I was on a plane to Vilnius, Lithuania with the Bernard Allison Group earning $1000 a week as the new drummer. I couldn't believe success tasted so sweet!

I know what you're thinking, $1,000 per week sounds good, right? Well, let's do the math, shall we? When I accepted the gig, I didn't negotiate. I didn't ask about daily per diem, how many shows we play a week, and so on. I was just happy to have an international touring gig. I quickly discovered that I was playing six nights a week, which comes to about $166 a night. Don't get me wrong, I still lived with my parents so the money sounded great over the phone. When I realized how demanding it was to play six nights a week, I felt under paid. I never told anyone this and I never complained. I knew I had a golden opportunity. I had enough money to move out of my parents' house, after about a year of touring.

I learned another lesson after my first year with Bernard, a $1000 per week is a livable wage if the band toured without long breaks. Bands may take a whole month off at a time a few times a year, not including the holiday season. So I had to go back to playing local clubs and bars to make ends meet. I felt ashamed going back to play bars. In my mind everyone on the scene thought I was in Europe touring. I thought playing local gigs would make me look like a failure but the truth was, nobody cared. Most Blues musicians that tour with big acts come back to their local gigs soon after the tours are over. After all, why not? It keeps your chops up and who doesn't like a $100 and a free meal. Playing locally also is great for networking to secure recording sessions. I get a lot of sessions like this. I ask the local musicians, who's making a record, and when? This became a steady balance throughout my career. Just because you tour, does not mean your local bar and club days are over. Vic Jackson was one of the musicians I called when I returned home letting him know my work availability. Vic had just got the gig as Ana Popovic's new bass player and because of his recommendation, she hired me to play drums.

In 2007, I began playing with Ana Popovic. Ana is a Serbian-born guitar player and singer-songwriter. While Bernard was on hiatus I toured the U.S with Vic and Ana, we were a power trio. I enjoyed playing her music and it was a change of pace for me. We toured throughout the summer and after the tour wrapped up, I toured Europe with Bernard. January of 2008, she offered me a permanent spot in her band. I had a conflicting feeling because of my loyalty towards Bernard. Plus I loved his music! However, Ana was offering me an apartment in Amsterdam and $200 a show. I figured I could earn more money and move to Europe, so I was all in. When I called Bernard to quit the band I felt guilty as if I was betraying him. I called and he didn't answer. I left a message and later an email. I gave him a month's notice to find a drummer. Looking back on it now, I think about how nervous I was to quit a band and start over again with a new artist. I never thought Ana was a bigger star than Bernard. In fact Bernard is a large reason for Ana's success. He helped her get her first record deal. I joined Ana's band because I wanted to earn more money and travel new places. Ana had a smaller band and less road expenses, so she could afford to pay me a little more than Bernard. Ana had an Eastern Europe and U.S following, plus she toured more often than Bernard. At that time Bernard toured western Europe, Scandinavia, Northern Africa and the United States. Every act has a different fan base and places they call home. When you are a side-musician you experience the artist perks not the struggles they went through to achieve it. You bypass the long van rides or empty late bars they had to play on the way up the success ladder. When I was with Bernard I rode on a fancy tour bus, and stayed at 4 and 5-star hotels. Ana hadn't built her business to that point just yet. She was traveling in rental vans, and staying in cheap motels. I knew through her work ethic and voluminous schedule she was bound to change that.

When I left Bernard's band to join Ana's I went through a transition from being an up-and-coming musician to a veteran.

My attitude changed negatively. In the following chapter I will discuss how it affected my career.

CHAPTER 2

Be Nice

During my early years with Bernard Allison I was nice to fans and respectful to bandmates. In January 2008, I moved to Amsterdam and joined the Ana Popovic Band and my attitude changed. I became arrogant, complacent, egotistical and I abused weed and alcohol daily. Ana's sister had moved to Spain temporarily to live with her boyfriend leaving her apartment abandoned. So Ana gave me a key to her flat. I had a new gig, I was living rent-free, and I was earning money but I thought drinking and using drugs was expected of a touring musician. My off days in the band worked like this: I woke up, smoked weed, and listened to the last show played by the band. I recorded most of our shows with my portable digital recorder. This allowed me to listen to song tempos and my drum solo. (I was all about a drum solo in those days.) Then I visited coffee shops, smoked more weed, and played pool with the locals. After a few games I walked around the city to explore. Amsterdam is beautiful and great for walking. After my walks I went back to the apartment, ate, watched t.v., smoked more weed, and napped. In the evening I got dressed went out and partied. I wasn't taking drum lessons, sticking to a real practice schedule, writing or studying new music. I was complacent, and I really didn't care much about music anymore. I cared about the lifestyle. I wanted to play drums so I could afford to party in Amsterdam.

I didn't realize I lost touch with my family and friends back home. I didn't call home as much, I didn't care to speak to my friends, I was selfish. On work days, I had to meet the band either at the airport or Ana's house prior to traveling. I was always late and hung over. When you spend your nights drinking and partying your mornings suffer. I didn't speak much in the mornings. I just held myself together long enough to get on the plane. Sometimes I could hardly stand up straight. When I flew, I snored loudly and the flights never felt long enough. We played other European cities on the weekends and I didn't take advantage of all the site seeing opportunities I had. I just nursed my hangovers in the hotels until sound check, where I became alert and focused. I had too, after all it was my job. Some days I was cordial to the bandmates, and there were some when I was rude. Ronald Yonker was the bass player. Ronald is from Groningen Holland and is one of the nicest guys I have ever met. I never have seen him lose his temper, and he handled his hangovers with class (He didn't complain about his whiskey headaches.) He always had a bright smile and highly energetic. He did back flips in the dressing room before gigs and whatever else to avoid a bored moment. His bass playing was great, and his stage presence mimicked a rock star, not a Blues man. Michelle Poppadia was a keyboardist from Florence Italy and was a consummate professional. He didn't speak much English, so he communicated through his body language and smile. Michelle traveled with us mostly in Europe. We had another keyboardist in the U.S named James Pace. James was a proud Roanoke Virginian and he was restless. He was the type of guy always out of the van first, and in the hotel check in line. If you want to reserve a table at a restaurant you send James. If you want to get the van packed up fast after a gig, trust me James is on it. James once got his finger caught in an elevator loading the band gear. He didn't cry about it, he just wrapped it and finished the tour. For a keyboard player, your fingers are everything and he proved he has tough character. Tony Basil was our road manager. He was from Indianapolis Indiana and had the greatest stories. These were my bandmates and its a shame I didn't talk to them much until after soundcheck. I got angry when the band turned a 30 minute soundcheck into a 2 hour rehearsal. I wanted to go back to the hotel, eat, sleep and rid my headaches before the show. I thought that soundcheck shouldn't be rehearsals which in almost every case, it is.

Soundcheck is a part of the job every musician, no matter the tier of success does. If you want to keep the gig, you must handle sound-checks in a pro manner. If you are hung over in a sound-check (which I advise against), no one should know. You must realize that if you drink too much alcohol on tour, you will pay the price the next day. So, don't whine, don't complain or, ask for aspirin and coffee, just play your instrument with a big smile. I had to learn this the hard way. I withdrew myself from the band during the day, but after the gigs I was the biggest party animal. I was immature because I didn't realize, once you're on tour you are on the clock, on and off the stage. If a band leader wants to turn a soundcheck into a rehearsal, then that's just part of the job. While I was in Ana's band I was performing fine, but I was drinking too much. I wasn't handling sound-checks well, and I lacked respect for sound engineers, which is a big mistake.

The proper way to start a soundcheck is, introduce yourself to the sound engineer when you arrive. A sound engineer is hired exclusively by the venue to operate the sound equipment for the bands. They are responsible for making your performance sound great, but they don't exclusively work for you, so they are worthy of respect. Never tune drums or alter anything onstage without asking permission of the sound engineer first. Another mistake I made was, I got frustrated with sound engineers when I played overseas because of the language barriers. This was a stupid mentality. When you are a guest abroad you should always try to speak the local language, because you are the foreigner. It helps to learn a few words of language used in the country you are touring. When I toured with Bernard Allison Group, and Ana Popovic Band we performed a lot in Germany. Later in my career I learned phrases like, "Hello my name is" and "Do You Have?" in German just to be able to break the ice. Once I learned this, I got better responses from the sound engineers, which in turn made for a better show.

During my time in the Ana Popovic Band I became overzealous. I felt obligated to add my opinion's in all band discussions which sometimes turned into arguments. These matters ranged from restaurant choice for dinner, to the show's set-list order. When Ana changed song tempos abruptly during our performances I didn't adjust. I started playing to a metronome on the shows just so I wouldn't have to take direction from her live on stage. When Ana wanted me to sing unison with the band, I refused. I maintained a defiant attitude because I lacked confidence in my singing. The correct way to respond to these situations is simple. When asked what you would like to eat, be open to what everybody wants unless it's your birthday. When it's time to discuss the setlist, listen to everyone's opinion, give yours, and remember the final decision isn't up to you. If you are asked to change the way a song is played just do it, in rehearsal and live. When Ana asked me to sing, instead of being self-conscious I should have just done my best. Sometimes an extra voice is needed in a song to make it's chorus obtuse. In the present stage of my career I sing with various acts and I don't think I sound good at all, but I sing loud and proud when asked.

When I began touring with Ana, I didn't listen to the lyrics of the songs. I just learned the drum parts in her music. One day I listened to her album "Hush." I noticed through the hard guitar riffs, where some lyrics about love and heartbreak. While on tour, I asked her about her life and travels which, provides the bulk of her songwriting content. Ana is from Belgrade, Serbia where she grew up during the Milosevic regime. Ana moved to Holland, toured Europe playing Blues, got married, and later moved to the United States. Her songs are a reflection of her past. When I understood this, I was able to connect with the music, thus making the shows better. I understood the message in the lyrics, so I adjusted my playing. I stopped playing drum fills and cymbal crashes in the verses of her songs. When you take on a new gig, it is important to get acquainted with the artist as best as you can. If you don't understand the message and lyrics of songs, you should ask. You may get some great stories out of the conversation. Every song begins with a thought or experience.

At this point of my career I was solidifying my place in Ana's band but I didn't know the importance of a luxury we all have, and that is time. Managing your time in all things is very important in the music business and the following chapter further explains this.

CHAPTER 3

The Rules Of Time

Time is very important to a professional musician and so is practice. I will explain how they correlate. I believe a musician should practice the same time of day or close to it as much as possible. Practicing the same time daily lets the people in your life know to respect that time. You don't want to get in the mood to practice, sit with your instrument and 2 minutes into a groove your mate asks, "Honey can you go to the store?" If you practice the same time daily your spouse would know to wait after your practice time to ask you to run an errand. Dedicate a practice time during the day when the living space is quiet and stick to it. Next, I will cover my method of practice.

In this present state of my career I maintain a daily practice log. This is valuable because there are plenty of days when I don't know what to practice. I don't feel inspired every day. When my creativity hits a wall, I can always go back in my log and practice some techniques I have abandoned in the past. I practice 2 1/2 hours daily and about 3 ½ when I'm preparing for a tour. When I first started committing to daily practice I didn't have the mental stamina to practice that long. I got distracted and stopped after about 30 minutes. This is common. A half-hour practice daily is better than none. It is really what you do with the time. If you start practicing with no plan then you are just *jamming*. Jamming, is playing something you already know for fun, but at some point you have to study. Studying is when you practice something you haven't mastered, methodically and slowly, for long periods of time. When I make a practice plan I allow time for jamming, which is during my first 10 minutes of practice. I spend this time warming up and just being a kid again. After my hands are loose I put my cell phone on airplane mode and I get to work. I spend the next 30-45 minutes sight reading. I am proud to share this with you. Reading is something I have been putting off until last year. (As I am writing this chapter its 2019). I got a phone call from my friend Kenny Coleman. Kenny is an incredible drummer, while talking, he asked if I could read music. I told him I could a little, but have been inconsistent and never get asked to read on my gigs. He said, "If you are a pro then there's no reason why you shouldn't be reading. You don't want to get a big offer and have to turn it down because you can't read a chart." He was right. After our talk I searched YouTube for some reading lessons and added them into my practice routine. Hopefully by the time you are reading this I will be a pretty good sight reader. After reading I spend about 20 minutes each on 3 or 4 drumming exercises. I work on 4-way independence, world rhythms, shuffles, and odd-time grooves. I work in increments of 20 minutes because it takes me 10 minutes to get the technique correct, and the next 10 minutes is dedicated to controlling my limbs and thoughts. I focus on the task at hand, and I avoid all distraction. After the 20 minutes is up and I feel satisfied with the results then I move on to the next exercise. Most of the rhythms I practice are not played on my gigs but it makes the gigs so much easier because of the muscle memory I've developed. I take a break after 90 minutes then practice another 60 minutes. I do this because, when you play bar and club gigs in Chicago the first set is 90 min and most headlining festival acts are 90 min as well. I use the break time to stretch, eat a snack, and check my physical mail. I don't check emails or turn on the television because the short break could lead into a long distraction so I keep it under 20 minutes. After my break I start the next faze of practice which is key to securing a gig for many years.

During the second half of practice I chart and play the songs that I perform live. If the upcoming gig is a reoccurring one then I play along with the pre-recorded rehearsal or show. I recommend keeping a recording device handy so anytime you play with a band in rehearsal or live show you can record, and then practice to the playback. Now that I've covered practice time, next, I will discuss punctuality.

Be on time for all of your gigs. Tardiness is one of the biggest reasons why musicians get fired. If you play drums locally, arrive at the venue at least one hour before showtime. This keeps the band leader from calling you wondering where you are. No band leader wants the stress of wondering if the drummer is going to be on time. I live in Bloomington Il. It's a 2 and half hour drive to most of my local gigs. If I have a 9:30 showtime in Chicago I must leave at 5:30. This gives me time to handle whatever mishaps that may occur on the way to the gig. Also, I arrive early to set up before the rest of the band, because it's easier on an empty stage. Another luxury of being early is, you won't have to stress over finding a parking spot.

Playing music in major cities can be a hassle when it comes to parking. On a 2019 gig in Nashville, I talked to famed songwriter John Hiatt about the downtown music scene. The biggest complaint he conveyed was parking. He told me how 10 years prior, "You could show up to your gig 20 min before showtime, park right in front of the bar, and walk into your gig stress free." Now that Nashville has grown in population, business has grown and downtown is overcrowded with tourist. Finding a park can be overwhelming, it could take over an hour to find street parking. When you are working in a big city you must watch or listen to traffic and whether reports the morning of your gig so you know when to leave home. Early arrival is important for setting up gear, and finding a park. Next, I will discuss how to take advantage of your spare time during gigs.

Whatever your habits are, do not try to feed them before the show. Going to the other side of town to visit a lover, taking a drive to score drugs, or a trip to the bootlegger for moon shine can wait till after the show. If you get caught in traffic or busted with drugs you can kiss your gig goodbye. Warming up on your instrument is recommended before your performance which I will discuss in detail later in Chapter 4.

If you play a gig with more than one set, you may be afforded a 30-minute break. During the set break, be mindful of your time. I go to my car and call my fiancé on my breaks. Before I leave the club, I ask the door attendant or stage manager what time are we back on stage? I arrive near the drums at least 5min before showtime if it's a small bar. If it's a big venue I'm backstage 10min before showtime just in case some new songs are added to the next set. If it's a first time hire I don't leave the venue at all. I talk to the band because this is a good time to network. Don't wait till after the gig to network because if they're good musicians, they're in demand and, If they're in demand, as soon as the last note is played on the gig, they're out the door fast. Now that I've discussed the importance of punctuality for playing locally, next I will discuss it for gigs that requires flying.

Arrive at the airport on time, which is 90 minutes before domestic flights and, 2 1/2 hrs before international. If you arrive just before takeoff, you may be permitted to board the flight but your checked bags may not, since checked baggage is loaded before passengers. Now that we covered airport punctuality, next I will discuss an important rule; don't get drunk the night before you fly.

If you abuse alcohol it can cause you to over sleep and miss your flight. During a tour in Ana Popovic's band we played a show in Oslo, Norway. The next morning we were going to fly separately to Los Angeles for two rehearsals, then on to Park

City, Utah to play an afterparty at the Sun Dance film festival. The movie, "What Love Is" starred Cuba Gooding Jr, Matthew Lillard, Gina Gershon, and Tamala Jones featured one of Ana's songs in the movie's sound-track which earned us an invitation to the premiere. The night before the flight from Oslo Norway to L.A to do all the aforementioned I did the dumbest thing ever. After the show in Norway there were free drinks at an after party and I got rock-star wasted. The next morning I woke up late, and terribly hungover. Ana's manager arranged a taxi to pick me up at 7am for a noon flight, and the airport was 2 hours away. You know your day is going to be bad when you wake up late and drunk, exclaiming, "Oh Shit." When I realized I overslept, I got out of bed, flung open the window drapes and noticed a taxi with it's engine running in the hotel parking lot. I ran downstairs dressed in my underwear, flagged the taxi driver and caught him just as he was pulling off. I told him I would be right back. I ran back up to my room, got dressed quickly, frantically packed my suitcase, and ran back down to the taxi. I forgot I stored my cymbal case in the hotel's front desk closet the night before, thinking it would be convenient to pick them up during hotel checkout. Well, alcohol doesn't enhance the memory, so in my hungover panicked state I left my cymbals. I fell asleep as soon as I got into the backseat of the taxi. When the driver woke me up at the airport I was so hungover it felt like I had the flu and I smelled bad because I didn't shower. I got out of the cab and the driver handed me my luggage when I realized I left my cymbals back at the hotel. I explained the situation to the driver and he assured me he had time to retrieve the cymbals before the flight. He warned me I would be cutting it close. I went into the airport and checked my luggage. I didn't go to the boarding area. Instead, I found an empty bench and feel asleep again. My inner clock woke me up just as I saw the driver running up to me with my cymbals. He passed me the cymbals and I ran over to the boarding gate. When I arrived at the gate the plane was gone. I put my hands on the window and fought back the tears. I had to sweat it out over the phone lying to Ana's manager saying it was a snow storm that made me miss the flight. That was another mistake I made. You should never lie in any situation, it just makes matters worse. I sat in the airport 24 hours and caught the next flight to Los Angelas. I made it to the second day of rehearsal, which costed Ana more money. She hired Tony Braunagel whom co-produced and played on her previous record to substitute the rehearsal I missed. I could have lost my gig at that point but thank God Tony was already booked so he couldn't take the Utah gig. We flew to Park City, Utah the next day and on the plane I sat next to Darryl Hannah (starred in the movie 1980s hit movie Splash). I got to Utah, played the gig and partied with movie stars. I hadn't learned my lesson. I was rewarded for my irresponsible behavior. And unfortunately I continued to gambled with my career. I was offered the chance of a lifetime and I could have ruined it due to drinking. I was fortunate I didn't lose my gig, but I was close. Now that I've covered the importance of being sober the night before you fly, next I will discuss being on time for *lobby call*.

 Be on time for *lobby call*. Now this rule is simple, but I must confess, I'm still working on it. Lobby call is when the band and road manager meet in the lobby of a hotel prior to leaving for airports, sound-checks, and shows so every group member is counted for. The first time I missed lobby call in Bernard's band I almost had a heart attack. It was 2005, my first international tour and we were 2 days in. I had never travelled abroad so jet lag was a new feeling. We were somewhere in eastern Europe and we had a bus call of 4 o'clock to go to soundcheck. Since we had a tour bus there was no lobby call, you just showed up on the bus and Dave the tour manager did a head count. The curtain on my bus bunk was closed. Dave thought I was in my bunk sleeping so he didn't check my bunk as to not to disturb me. Dave counted me as present and told the driver to leave for the gig. I was in my hotel room getting the best sleep I had since arriving in Europe. I wanted to make a good impression on the band but I was late for work on the second of a 30-day tour. Dave Brown is not the type of tour manager you want to upset. He's serious about everything concerning Bernard Allison. When the bus drove about a mile from the hotel he realized I wasn't on the bus so they made a U-turn. When I heard Dave pounding on my hotel door I woke up thinking I was in a drug raid. With my heart racing I looked around wondering, where was I? Dave was yelling on the other side of the door, "Wake up, your fucking late." I opened the door in my sleepy haze and he nonchalantly stated, "Get your sticks and get on the fucking bus we got to go." That is when I realized, I was on a European tour with a Blues-Rock band. I got on the bus with the embarrassing look of shame. The best thing to do in a situation like this is apologize to everybody and try not to make the mistake twice on the same tour.

 Adjusting to tour life isn't easy, especially your first year. You must get used to moving to a daily schedule, and sometimes your bowels don't agree. I've had times when I'm almost to the elevator on my way downstairs to make lobby call and I must go back to my room to use the bathroom. This can make you minutes late, and in some bands, it can cost you a gig. I learned over the years to wake up early on tour, workout if a hotel gym is provided, eat, and take care of your morning business. When you wake up early you don't leave items behind. I've left stage clothes and shoes in closets, travel pillows, bathroom bags, cell phone chargers and leftovers in hotel refrigerators all because I was rushing to make lobby call. Another rule of time concerns the recording studio.

Be on time to the recording studio. This rule is important because it is costly to be late. Most studio's in Chicago rent for about $40 to $65 an hour. If you play a melody instrument and you get a call for a session, show up an hour early. This should give you time to load in your instrument and find parking. If you play drums, show up 2 hours early. Drums take the most time before a session. You must tune, let the engineer add microphones to your drums and check the sound. If there is any squeaks or rattles coming from the drums you must get rid of it fast. I encourage keeping DW-40 and gaff tape in your drum pedal case. DW-40 is a degreasing spray that's great for eliminating squeaks from your drum hardware. The drum and microphone check other-wise known as *getting sounds* may take anywhere between 20 minutes to 1 hour, if things are going smooth. To *get sounds*, you must put on headphones and strike the drums separately to make sure each microphone is getting a signal. While you are doing this the engineer is listening in the control room to make sure the drum kit is tuned properly and for any unwanted sounds. After you are completely set, and your headphones are adjusted, you may be asked to play a beat. Play spacious and controlled. Avoid playing fancy licks and chops. Play the grooves you are going to use in the songs for that session. After getting sounds, go into the control room and listen to your drumming through the speaker monitors. Listen carefully to make sure all the drums are tuned. Now that we have our drum sounds adjusted to the sound engineer's approval we are ready to record. Next, I will discuss how time is important in executing music.

Be on time, *in the music* while recording, which means use a metronome if asked. If you are a drummer, you will be asked to play to a metronome, and this shouldn't be a problem. Daily practice to a metronome will prepare you for this, which brings me to my next rule. Practice the music before the recording session if it is available, so it can go as smooth as possible.

When you are hired to play on someone's record there is a lot of trust involved. The artist trusts that you are going to show up with a pro attitude and deliver. Delivering is about giving the artist the best experience musically and in a timely fashion. Remember when you are in the studio, you are on the clock, so arrive prepared. If the music arrangements change from what was originally sent, a valuable studio musician can make music adjustments on the fly, chart a new arrangement quickly, and follow any directions given without long discussion.

In 2009, I inadvertently received a costly lesson taught by my mentor Tony Braunegel. Tony is a sweetheart and master musician. I was in Calabasas, California working on Ana Popovic's "Blind for Love Album" and Tony was the co-producer. While recording the song "More than Real," the producer David "Z" wanted a different feel for the song. David "Z" is known for his work with Prince on his 1986 hit, "Kiss" and many more chart toppers. The recording session felt like an on the spot math quiz, and I was failing miserably. I played this song live several times on the road with Ana but the producer wanted to me to change my approach. After a few unsuccessful attempts "Z" said that my ideas sounded, "Too busy." Tony strolled over to the drums and asked if he could give it a try. I retreated to the control room as Tony sat down and got adjusted. David "Z" started the track and Tony started playing a simple pattern on the snare drum using the brushes. He turned the snares off on the drum so it sounded smooth. I stood and watched through the control window with my arms folded thinking, *damn I wish I would have thought of that.* I thought Tony was giving me rhythm ideas, so afterwards I could record my own version. I realized that ship had sailed when Grammy award winning producer David "Z" clapped his hands and said, "Wow, that's the take." I had to hide my jealousy and embarrassment when Tony returned to the control room to a cheering mini-audience including my boss, Ana Popovic exclaiming "Bravo Tony, way to save the day!" I smirked and clapped too. I lost $150 in 3 minutes and 14 seconds, the time it took Tony to record the song and get my fee. This experience taught me to practice multiple styles of music so I can quickly adjust to a producers request. Tony had been studying and recording drums for many years so when the music required a different feel Tony could adjust quickly, and I couldn't. Now that I've explicated time as it pertains to music, and the importance of studying multiple styles of music, let's discuss mentally preparing for a gig.

CHAPTER 4

Warm Up

When you practice, play a gig, or record, approach it with peace and mental clarity. Never put yourself in a bad situation before you play.

In 2007, I played a show in Vaasa, Finland with the Bernard Allison Group. Before the show, I walked through the crowd and saw a lady standing at a table by herself so I started a conversation. We talked for a few minutes and before I could say goodbye, a man at the table next to ours smoking a wooden pipe walked over. He was a tall, old grey-haired man with a thick mustache, wearing a fringed motor cycle jacket, a plaid shirt with a turquoise boa, and black faded jeans. He resembled an extra for the 1969 film "Easy Rider." He looked me square in the eye, turned to the lady across from me and dumped his ashes right into her beer. He gave us both the stink eye and turned away like nothing ever happened. It took great restraint not to attack him and start a bar fight. I envisioned myself giving him a Mike Tyson's style upper cut. Instead, I was temporarily speechless, and the woman was visibly hurt. She was a medical student from Ghana, and she warned me in our short chat that blacks were not welcomed in Finland. Ironically, the guy proved her words to be true. After the initial shock wore off, I started yelling at the guy which started a commotion. Security came over and stood between us. They exchanged a few words in Finnish with the Dennis Hopper look-a-like, and then escorted me backstage. I was in disarray when I realized, I must entertain this rude guy because he was never escorted out of the venue. Instead he went back to his table after talking with security, like nothing ever happened. I told Dave, our tour manager what happened expecting him to get security to throw him out. Instead Dave annoyingly looked at me and said, "Why the fuck were you out there anyway? We got a fucking show to play!" and walked away. That was it, and he was right. If I was backstage listening to the pre-recorded show or, warming up on my practice drum pad instead of patrolling the venue socializing, I would have never been in that situation.

    Warming up is very important because it loosens you up. I play with my friend Dave Herrero and the Hero Brothers. Dave opens his show with an up tempo *jump shuffle*, a beat found in west-coast Blues. Most Chicago players never explore this style and Dave is a master at it. When I started playing with Dave, I wasn't warming up before the show. The first song was always a challenge because of the fast tempo. I started cold and played too hard because, I was tensing my muscles. This caused me to *fight* the drum-set, bashing and crashing trying to keep up. In order to play well you must warm up before the gig, not during it. Don't use the first 3 songs of the set to get warmed up, instead warm up backstage or somewhere isolated for twenty minutes prior to the show, so if the band leader calls out an uptempo song you will be ready. Sometimes you may be required to play an opening instrumental with a solo section, warming up prepares you for it. Next, I will explain how I warmup.

Before I perform I practice on my drum pad to the metronome app on my phone. I practice drum rudiments to various tempos that I play during the show. After practicing rudiments, I listen to the songs I play in the show and groove to them. If the dressing room is full, I use a pillow instead of my drum pad so, I don't disturb anyone. Nobody wants to be around a drummer backstage hitting a hard surface with sticks, its annoying. Warming up when you are working with a new artist is important because it makes you look serious. I'm impressed when I see a master musician prepare. It lets me know no matter who you are, we all must prepare and, warming up is part of the mental preparation.

During the summer of 2019, I played Cazorla, Spain's annual Blues festival with "Chicago Plays the Stones," a Rolling Stones cover band featuring Chicago Blues artist 3-time Grammy nominee harpist Billy Branch, guitarist Ronnie Baker Brooks, bassist Felton Crews, and keyboardist Darryl Counts. This was an all-star lineup. Most of the musicians on the festival stayed in the same hotel. I was watching TV in my hotel room when I heard some beautiful saxophone riffs in the distance. I went downstairs and to my surprise Maceo Parker was in the hotel dining room all alone, practicing. I looked through the glass doors as he paced in circles playing scales. He stopped every few minutes to dump the saliva from his horn, then more blowing and pacing. Maceo has played with legends from James Brown to Prince and he still practices and warms up, the way we all should. I went to his concert that night. I was backstage hanging out before they went on, and I could hear those same scales in the distance of his dressing tent. Maceo was warming up, and when he got on stage he was on fire! In the next chapter, I will discuss when it's appropriate to cancel a gig, the importance of sounding authentic, the meaning of double-dipping, musicians dress-code, and the importance of respecting an artist platform.

CHAPTER 5

Respect The Gig

You must respect every gig offered to you. Remember, when an artist calls you, it is your skill and reputation that got you the call. In order to keep your reputation intact you must show up when called.

When I commit to a local gig, I never cancel it to play with another artist, even if I'm offered more money. If another artist calls and I'm already booked, I thank the artist for considering me and let them know that I am looking forward to working with them in the future. I keep the original gig and I never mention the more lucrative offer to the band or artist that I kept the date with. I do not convey the aforementioned because that belittles the artist. However, if I get a call from an artist for a lucrative international tour that may result in long term job security then I will call the artist and cancel the gig. When I cancel, I don't provide an explanation because the artist may feel slighted, but I do provide a substitute. I let them know the sub is expecting their call. If the gig is two weeks away then this usually works out o.k. This policy is also good for networking, because the unwritten rule amongst working musicians is; if a musician refers you for a gig, you owe them one. Thats how I maintain work. I have four drummers that I call for gigs when I need a sub, and they call me in return. When I recommend a musician for a gig and they don't return the favor, I do not recommend them anymore. Subbing out a local gig occasionally is fine when you are in demand and you have established good relationships with multiple artists. But even established veterans must follow this next rule.

When an artist buys you a plane ticket. You must play the gig, even if you receive a more lucrative offer. I never advise any musician to cancel a gig after the artist already spent money on plane tickets, especially international flights. Even though a flight can be changed, and you could reimburse the changing fees, the artist will still resent you for cancelling. Hotels, marketing merchandise, band photos, and a whole lot more may have to be changed if you cancel, resulting in you having contentions with the artist. The rumors will spread about how you cannot be trusted which may take years to correct. Next, I will introduce you to a word coined by Dave Herrero, the "Double dip."

Don't *double dip,* unless you got time to make the trip. "Double Dipping" is a term my friend Dave Herrero and I came up with one night. We were talking about how it's tough to make a club gig after a performance at Navy Pier. Navy Pier is a tourist area in Chicago, known for its giant Ferris wheel adjacent to Lake Shore Drive. They have bands during the summer, and the last set is over just before 9p.m. This gives a sliver of a chance to drive to Kingston Mines, B.L.U.E.S. on Halsted, or Buddy Guys Legends, find parking, and start a 9:30 set, on time, even though the venues are less than 10 miles away. The traffic is congested downtown, especially on weekends because of the tourists. If you arrive at a gig, punctual, under those circumstances, you are *double dipping*. When you book two gigs on the same day with two different artists you must be careful. I know some veteran Chicago drummers who have mastered the art of the double dip. Drummers go to the club they are performing at 9:30pm early, usually around 5p.m. and assemble a drum kit. Then take another drum kit to their early afternoon gig. This way they can avoid the set-up time, walk right into the club at 9:30 and start drumming without a minute to spare. They use valet service if available so they don't waste time searching for parking. Double-dippers have hired me to cover the first set of their gigs. They arrived on the second set, paid me $50 and they finished out their night. Some of these drummers didn't tell their bandleader they weren't playing the first set, which placed me in some awkward positions. I don't conduct my business this way. I don't like the stress of it all so I don't recommend it. I turn down late gigs all the time if I have an early afternoon one because you never know how long the gig will last. Just because the gig is supposed to be over at 9pm doesn't mean you will leave at 9pm. Circumstances may occur like; the band wanting to extend the set because somebody dropped a $100 in the tip jar, the venue is extremely crowded and the load out is almost impossible, or the artist simply made a mistake with how many sets the band must play. I've been through all of this and the outcome is the same. Neither artist cares about your reasons for leaving early or showing up late. They want you to do the job they are paying you for, so I don't recommend double dipping. Next, I will discuss how this correlates with festivals hosting multiple artist.

Festival *double dipping* is o.k. if the performance times do not overlap, and the artist is in agreement with it. I've been on some festivals headlining with an artist and the opening act needs a drummer. When I get an offer to play with another band on the same show it's normally because the drummer abruptly cancelled. I always ask permission of the artist I am there with first if I could play with another artist, and I explain the situation. If the permission is granted then I will play the set, if not I don't and, I never mention it again as it may lead to a dispute. If I am permitted, I charge the band I am subbing for the same amount of money they would have paid their drummer. Subbing for another band is a great way to begin musical relationships. If you accept the same pay as the absent band member, the artist may look at it as a favor. Favors like this can result in future work with the artist or whomever they tell of your good deeds. If you overcharge a desperate artist, it's a business deal that will end in a one time transaction. I follow these rules of asking permission and charging fair rates because it is my way of showing respect. When I ask permission to play with another artist on the same lineup, I really don't have to, but I respect the fact I would not be on the show in the first place if they had not hired me. If asking is uncomfortable with you then at least alert them of your decision to play with another artist and if asked why, explain. Next, I will discuss respect, as it relates to the music you are hired to play.

Respect the music. If you did not write it, perform it as close to the way it is originally recorded. Try not to change anything unless you are asked. Artist spend a great amount of time writing songs and they deserve to hear their songs performed as they intended. Also, stay respectful to the genre you are hired to play. If the genre is Blues, play the Blues, if the genre is Jazz do the same. Don't be the Gospel-sounding musician on a Blues gig. This is the main reason why some Chicago drummers never make it past playing the bars. I have seen some drummers play Blues even though they hate it. They try to play it because of the "easy money," but then they get replaced because they do not sound authentic.

Blues music sounds simplistic but, in order to be a great Blues player, you have to put the same time and energy into it as you put in any other style of music. Blues music requires *Pocket* playing. *The Pocket*, is a term that basically means, repeating the beat in-time and playing nothing else. Playing *the pocket* and sounding involved is a technique that keeps a drummer working consistently. The story I will share next elucidates this.

In 2010, I toured and recorded with Mississippi Heat. Mississippi Heat is a traditional Blues band with a rich history extending back to the 1990s. Every album and live show is dedicated to 1950s and 60s style Chicago blues. The bandleader Pierre Lacocque, a Belgian-born harmonica master writes the songs and hires a female vocalist to front the band. I was a substitute drummer for Grammy award winner Kenny "Beady Eyes" Smith who had been in Mississippi Heat many years prior to me working with the band. When I first started playing with Mississippi Heat the music sounded easy to play but, it wasn't. The first tour throughout Europe I tried playing the songs my way, but it wasn't the right feel for the music. I sat in my hotel room after the gigs and really studied Kenny's playing. I mimicked his swishy loose hi hat sound, and applied some pocket. A year later I became the main drummer for the band resulting in recording three albums on Delmark records. Pierre hired me permanently because I complemented his vocalist Inetta Visor, by playing in the pocket. I respected the gig by recognizing Kenny's contribution to Mississippi Heat and fused his style into my playing as well. When I first got the tour with Mississippi Heat I thought my approach was correct for the gig. But it was too contemporary. I was playing grooves and applying chops that supported my ego not the music. Egos are common in the music business but are not tolerated very long. A big ego can cause you to lose a gig, and the way to fan a musicians ego is give them a solo. Next, I will discuss a rule that pertains to this.

Don't ask for a solo. However, if one is offered then oblige. When you ask for a solo, you are asking a lot. You are asking an artist to trust in your ability to play all by yourself under pressure and entertain an audience. Some do it great, most do it just o.k. You must realize, you are consuming time from the show dedicated to the artist that wrote the songs and worked their whole life to be in that position, to feed your own ego. When you ask for a solo on a show that's all it is, ego. The best way to receive a solo is from request by the bandleader or the audience. I love it when the bandleader had no plans of giving me a drum solo, but the audience exclaims, "Give the drummer some." The best part about it is, I didn't have to ask. The paying customer asked for me, and they are always right. When you solo, the spotlight is on you so you want to look good, which is covered in my next rule; *Dress for the gig.*

What I wear to work is very important to me because I have pride in my appearance. I was raised that way. When I was a child, every Sunday morning I woke up to my Dad getting dressed in my room. My father stored his dress clothes in my closet. He owned over 30 suits, with beautiful matching shoes, with the biggest tie and hanker chief collection I'd ever seen. I watched him shine his shoes and tie his long silk neckties. He wore matching pocket squares. He was a minister and he took pride in the way he dressed. He taught me, always look your best. This advice would serve me well throughout my career.

In 2019, I arrived at a local gig wearing black shiny dress shoes, jet black creased Levi's, grey v-neck t-shirt and a black sports coat. I was wearing my diamond ring I inherited from my father and a gold watch my fiancé bought me for Fathers Day. I looked casual cool. I was hired by Chicago Blues harmonica player Omar Coleman to play "Smoke Daddies," a local BBQ restaurant and Blues hangout. I thought I dressed down, turns out to them I was dressed up. I walked in to the gig to the band saying, "Damn you must have just left a corporate gig." I said, *No I wore this for you, out of respect for your gig.* Omar smiled and said, "Now that's what I'm talking about."

When you play traditional-Blues the dress code is very old-school. The Chicago Blues artist I perform with require me to look my best. No gym shoes, blue-jeans, or baggy sweaters. The old school Blues men *dress to the 9s*. Nice suits and alligator shoes, fresh haircuts and shaves, shiny jewelry, and a clean car in the parking lot. This is the look of success for a Blues man. As for women the same rule applies, look your best. Every band doesn't take on this tradition, but I love it. When I began my career I didn't understand the Blues dress-code or the seriousness of my job until my first theater gig.

In 2003, I had my first gig with Liz Mandville Greeson and the Blue Points. Liz offered me a show at the Park-West theater in Chicago, a real classy venue. I was new to the Blues and I didn't know about her dress code. When I accepted the gig, it didn't occur to me to ask what to wear. I showed up wearing a red Durag, XX-L red and white t-shirt, blue jeans, and patent leather red Nikes. My Nikes were brand-new and my outfit matched. I looked like an extra for a Tu-Pac video but I thought I looked good. We had a sound check and the band had on their street clothes. 20 minutes before the show they went to separate dressing rooms and changed. The band came out dressed eloquent. Liz wore a fancy dress with sequence and fringes, and high-heel shoes. Dave K the bassist wore black slacks, white dress shirt with an ascot, and cool black shades. The guitarist Mike Gibb wore a purple shirt and a black tie, black slacks and beautiful snake-skin boots. Liz looked at me and asked, "Where's your stage clothes honey? It's almost showtime." I realized I was terribly under dressed and I could have crawled under a rock. It never occurred to me to dress up. I approached the stage timid because it was my first gig with the band, and my first time playing in a big theater. To make matters worse I felt embarrassed because of my appearance. My rule is, if you play Gospel, Jazz, Blues, Soul, or R&B dress up. If you aren't sure, ask the bandleader when you accept the gig. You can also go on YouTube and look at the band perform and dress accordingly. You want to look like you belong in the band, so dress the part. Now that we understand how appearance matters in terms of respecting the gig lets discuss an unwritten rule of respect. This rule deals with the principles of earning extra money on the gig.

Don't sell personal merchandise unless you have permission from the artist. An artist fanbase takes great effort to build so contentions may start if you sell your personal merchandise on their platform. Respect the gig and ask. My next rule covers selling the most important commodity, you.

Don't promote your side projects on someone else's gig. When you are a side-musician, you are supporting an artist dream. When an artist is enjoying the fruits of their labor by entertaining a packed house, the last thing they want is a musician they hired promoting a gig they have nothing to do with.

Some years ago I was backstage after playing a great set with a band. The guitar player and I were starting our nightly celebration, when a gentleman introduced himself. He said he was a local concert promoter and he loved our show. The guitar player told him about his band back home, how great they were, and he needed to hear them. He talked about his band so much he didn't notice our bandleader was staring with piercing eyes across the room. He sat there and watched the guitarist brag saying, "If you want to hear some real deal Blues, you got to hear my guys." It was total disrespect. I started doing my best version of Michael Jackson's moon walk, slowly back-pedaling away from the promoter and braggart musician. I didn't want to be guilty by association. After the tour he was fired with no explanation, but I knew why. The next rule of respect involves guest and friends of the band.

Ask permission before you bring a guest on tour. This rule is important because it's about respect. When you are hired to go on tour, remember it's not your tour. The only person allowed to bring guest without an explanation is the bandleader.

They may bring family, friends, and even pets, because they are the boss and they can do whatever they want. Now you on the other hand, is a different story. If you bring a spouse on tour your band-mates may see it as, less room in the van, an extra snorer on the tour bus, or an extra complainer in the backstage catering line. This may be fine for 2 days but 3 is pushing it. Some bands have musicians with bad attitudes. They may have night time habits that make them cranky during the day. Do you really want a hungover artist snarling at your partner because they are two minutes late to the bus? Something to think about before inviting your partner on tour with you. If you are going to do it, I suggest mapping out your own mode of transportation. Rent a car and trail the bus, and eat separately from the band unless invited to dinner. Eating separately eliminates the confusion over whether spouses are eating free from the band menu. Music venues have band menus to prevent bands from ordering expensive foods like steaks and lobsters. They offer the cheapest foods, a house salad, burger, wings, or cup of soup. You would think a club or theater wouldn't care if the drummer's partner had a few wings on the house, well think again. Not only does the club get annoyed, your band members might too. Faces get all awkward when it's time to tip the waitress. It's something about the bands spouses and a free meal that can get people all riled up. So many classless spouses have really spoiled the scene, they eat and drink top shelf alcohol all night without tipping. My fiancé Dr. Dawn Beichner is an accomplished Professor at Illinois State University, she makes a good living. So, just to avoid the confusion we sit at our own table and we pay for our own food. When I play the Legendary Rhythm and Blues Cruise I love to bring her because we do not have to travel with the band. We can enjoy each other without the stress of following a tour schedule. She pays for her flight. I pay for her cruise cabin fees, meals and port fees which is extracted from my pay, and it is a done deal. The cruise is 7 days, I play 4-75 minute shows and the rest of the time is ours. Even though we are not in the way of any band-members, I still ask for permission from the band leader before I bring her, out of respect.

Never bring your partner to the recording studio, unless it's your project or an extended invitation was given. Most artists do not want anybody to hear or see their creative process other than the parties directly involved when they are recording. So do not bring an entourage to the studio. I have worked in some small studios with tiny control rooms with just enough room for the engineer and maybe three other people. You do not want your friends or partner taking up seating when it is time for the band to listen to the playbacks. It could get awkward when the bandleader asks your partner to move to another room or please be quiet so we can listen to the recordings. Any distraction during the recording process is unwanted so come alone and ready to work. Now that we covered the rules of respect in the workplace, next I will discuss stage presence.

CHAPTER 6

Have Stage Presence

Chapter 6: Have Stage Presence

It is a warm feeling when I walk onto a theater stage and the audience breaks into applause before I have played a single note. There are not too many jobs where you receive an applause just for showing up. There are ways to walk onstage so you look cool, even though it may be your first major show and you are a nervous wreck. Before you start the show, ask the bandleader if the band is going to be introduced to the crowd by a master of ceremony. If the M.C calls out the band members individually, then walk out when your name is called, otherwise walk out in order of your instruments. The person with the instrument furthest away should go first and so on. This looks very smooth and organized to the audience. If you must sit at your instruments while the MC gives some announcements to the audience, this is a good time to make sure your instrument is turned on, or tuned and ready to go. I take this time to turn on the strainer on my snare drum, check to make sure my phone is on airplane mode, check my metronome app on my phone (a metronome serves as a guide for beat per minutes of a song), adjust my headphones, and make sure my set list is visible and taped down. I tape my setlist to a music stand because I use a fan and the tape will prevent it from blowing away. After my tools are in place and the drumsticks are in my hand, I look at the bass-player and smile. At this point I'm ready to play the down-beat of the opening song. I look at the bassist before I start the music because, the bassist and the drummer work together to form the rhythm section, we complement each other.

Smiling is a very important part of my stage presence. Smiling on the drums is a result of a positive attitude. I am happy to be there. I do not enjoy watching a band that is not having a good time. I love it when a band is intense, and happy. I don't need to hear jokes from the band. I just need to know they love what they are doing. You can achieve this by the way you play your instrument. You do not have to smile. If smiling is not your thing, then just make me feel it. Frown, growl, spit, whatever, be yourself times 10! It can be very hard to do this on the 3rd set of a late-night gig. I play the Kingston Mines, a popular Chicago Blues club. The gig starts at 10:30 p.m. and ends at 3:30 a.m. I could frown on the last set because my lower back hurts and I am sleepy. Or I could smile and play like it's Madison Square Garden. The latter is always the better because, you never know who's watching.

YouTube is another reason stage presence is important. We live in an era that everything you do can be recorded. I have had some rough gigs and, those moments are captured on someone's YouTube channel. When I smile, the audience isn't aware something is going wrong. My drum head could break, my sticks may fall out my hand, I may play a sour note, or the bass drum may slide away from me causing the pedal to disconnect from the drum-set. The viewer won't notice because of my reaction to the mishaps, a big grin. Training myself to smile when things go wrong on stage was not easy. Practicing in front of a mirror helped. It took a while to understand that it is ok if something goes wrong live. Just have fun and the audience will too. Another rule I will discuss involves alcohol.

Never drink alcohol onstage. This is a personal rule of mine. I refrain from using alcohol while performing because it can increase my chances of making a mistake. I am not as sharp and focused when I drink. I have never seen my drum hero's drink on-stage. Steve Jordan, Steve Gadd, Dennis Chambers, Bernard Purdie all may drink in their personal lives, but I have never seen it. They uphold a clean image and, I figure I should do the same. Bernard Allison told me long ago, "If you cannot wait 90 minutes to have a drink, then you have a serious problem."

Bernard had a strict rule in his band, "No drinking on-stage." I agree with him. I think drinking and performing is derived from playing the local bars and small clubs. Bar bands may drink and party all night, but struggle to get past that bar level in their careers. I have seen this on the Blues scene a lot of times. The band drinks alcohol, plays sloppy and loud, but yet they have big dreams of playing stadiums. It just does not work that way. One of the biggest reasons why bands stay in the bars forever is, they abuse alcohol which results in their show not being taken seriously. Some bands drink and enjoy the bar gigs because they are complacent in their careers. They do not believe they could evolve into a world-touring headlining act. They may take their musicianship seriously, but not the show. It is something about the vibe of a bar that can take the pride out of a serious musician, causing them to dumb down. These bands sometimes do well in packing the local bars. They may be content, living in the moment and having a barrel of laughs with drunk fans, but that lifestyle is not for me. I am not a weekend warrior playing for tips and free drinks. I am a world-class pro that practices very hard, so all the notes I play are important to me. They are not dulled by alcohol use, they are razor edge sharp. I encourage every musician to respect their craft as I do, if you want to elevate playing past the bar scene. Don't get me wrong about this rule. As I have said before it is a personal rule of mine. So there are exceptions.

Buddy Guy, and Lonnie Brooks (R.I.P.), are a few of my favorite Blues men I have seen drink responsibly on big stages. They have figured out how to incorporate alcohol in to their set for the image of having a great time. But I have never seen them drunk.

Lonnie Brooks was a legendary Blues performer from Louisiana. He performed with a water bottle of tea on his guitar amp. His drummer played a drum roll as he exclaimed to the crowd, "You see this bottle? It's full of Cognac." Then he guzzled the bottle, tossed it in the air and ripped into some guitar riffs, all to a screaming audience. I loved it! I thought it was really alcohol in the bottle until he told me later backstage it was just ice tea.

Grammy award winner Buddy Guy is the coolest of the living Bluesmen today. Buddy sits in with bands that play his club. I love it when he comes on-stage and sings. He performs a song, tells some Blues history, then orders a "Muddy Water" from the bar. That is the Blues slang for Cognac. He finishes up his Blues history lesson about John Lee Hooker, or T-Bone Walker with a drink of "Muddy Water" down the hatch. Then he goes into another song. His routine never gets old and I have seen it a hundred times. These guys are my exceptions to the rule. They mastered the art of entertaining. They had the illusion of the drinking Blues man but I have never seen them drunk. This next rule covers, noodling on your instrument, live. A mistake common amongst rookies.

Never noodle in between songs. I learned this from my friend Nigel Mack who is a Chicago Blues artist. We discuss music often and one thing he told me was "Blaze I cannot stand a noodling musician; the stage is no place to practice." He was right. If there is space between songs known as *dead air,* do not try to fill it up with your playing unless asked. Play only when the band plays. This will keep the audience engaged and hanging on your every note. The audience can become confused if you just start riffing on your instrument while the band leader is setting up for the next song. Sometimes an artist talks to the audience to introduce the band or explain the concept of the upcoming song. If you start playing your instrument during this time the audience may think the song is beginning, not understanding they are just listening to wasted notes. This next rule for drummers can be just as distracting as noodling. Turn off the strainer when the snare drum is not in use.

The strainer is a metal lever on the side of the snare drum that engages and disengages contact with the snares and the bottom head. When the snares are positioned tight against the drum it creates a rattling sound. The rattle can be heard through the venue, especially when the drum is amplified by microphones, which can create a distraction.

From 2014 to 2018 I performed with Kelly Hunt, a singer-songwriter from Lawrence, Kansas. Kelly explained the concepts of her songs prior to performing them throughout her set. When she talked, I turned off the snare strainer so the audience could hear her amplified voice without the rattle of my snare. Next, I will discuss performing despite having personal problems.

Leave your personal problems off stage. This rule is important because every musician has them. When you perform you must eliminate negative thoughts from your mind. I play concerts with a heavy head sometimes. All musicians do. But I smile and enjoy the music. One trick to doing this is, sing along to the words of the songs in your head. Think about the lyrics of the songs you perform. This keeps your brain distracted from personal problems. The next rule covers how side-musicians should handle contentions amongst each other.

Never argue on stage. By the time you are on stage, all grievances should be worked out. If you have a personal problem, give the band member a phone call and respectfully iron it out. Do not involve the band leader. Rehearsal is the place to address music related grievances with band mates but, not personal ones. If you are dissatisfied with the way your bandmates are executing the music, then you must address it respectfully. If you are in a band that does not rehearse, then sound check is a good place to iron out musical arrangements, but not personal problems.

The next rule should not have to be discussed. But I have seen so much of this in this business that I figured I better discuss it.

Never "clown around" onstage unless it is a part of the show. This is meant for the practical jokers, roasters, and back-stage party animals. Everyone loves a bandmate that is fun to get along with and a barrel of laughs. Especially when the tours are long. It is good to have a person in the group to break up the tension in disagreements, crack a good joke, and knows how to party responsibly. However, back-stage antics should not be carried onstage, all performances should be taken seriously. I will share a story with you that illustrates what can occur when band members do not approach their job seriously.

There is a talented drummer from Chicago that was fired for dancing inappropriately with the female lead singer during a show. The gig was almost over and the singer was introducing the band. When she got to the drummer he danced to the front of the stage and started humping her backside. It was in poor taste and the singer was embarrassed. The club banned the act from ever performing there again. When I heard the story, I was not shocked by this display of foolery. Situations like this happen when musicians take their gig for granted. Unfortunately the band lost a great opportunity because the drummer lacked self-control. Now that I have covered some stage rules, in the next chapter I will discuss musician post-show responsibilities. The perils of alcohol abuse. And how to network at an afterparty.

CHAPTER 7

After The Performance, What's Next?

After the encore of your last set, your job is not over. When I was in the Bernard Allison Group, and while I was performing European shows in the Ana Popovic band, my job after the show was to go to the merchandise table for the *meet and greet*. This is when an artist signs autographs, and take pictures with fans. After the meet and greet, I disassembled the drum kit so the stage hands could pack them for next day's travel. Afterwards I was done. I did not have to load any gear. This changed when I joined the Shawn Kellerman band.

In 2008, Shawn Kellerman, a Canadian Blues artist, saw my performance on Bernard Allison's DVD, "Energized Live in Europe" and gave me a call. Shawn was very direct. He told me he had tours booked throughout the States and was ready to record an album. I was excited for the opportunity. At the time I was unemployed. I just had my daughter Zoe, and I was getting over mourning the recent loss of my father. I had taken some time off the road and I was ready to get back to work. I met Shawn's bassist Joseph Veloz through the social media website, My Space. He contacted me before the tour and we became friends instantly. We were a power-house trio and we had a killer live show, without any rehearsals. I loved playing with that band. Every show we gave it our all. After our shows we did not have stage hands or roadies to pack our gear. We were independent artists. There was no budget for hiring roadies. This brings me to the next rule. Do not disappear when it is time to pack the van after the show.

When I toured with Shawn we did not have the luxury of stage hands. We carried our own gear and we mostly played bars. We went all over the country in an 18-passenger van. Shawn took out the back-row seats to fit the gear. At the end of each gig Joe and I had to pack the van while Shawn was getting paid. We had a game of physical Tetris down tight. We carried several guitars, a pedal board, 3 amps, bass pedal board, bass guitar, drum set, P.A., and luggage. This was a tough job some nights. Try carrying all of that gear from the stage, out of the front door of a crowded bar. Walking through a maze of drunk people patting you on the back while carrying a bass amp could be an Olympic competition. The #1 rule of the Olympic event would be not to drop the amp on anybody's foot. However, loading gear out of a packed bar feels better than loading out of an empty one.

I remember we had an early Sunday gig in St. Paul Minnesota. The load in was extremely tough. We had to carry our gear up two flights of stairs. Nobody came to the show so we played to the staff. The load out was depressing. Touring in the winter through Colorado was worse. At the Little Bear Saloon in Evergreen, Colorado we played to 2 people in a bar plus the staff and we were contracted for two nights. The same attendance showed up the second night, and after the show we had to load out the gear in three feet of snow. This was another depressing load out. The Motel 6 we stayed in that night made matters worse. It was freezing in our room due to the outside winds blowing through the air-conditioning vents. Joe and I slept fully clothed in our coats, winter hats, and boots. The room was so tiny I could reach my hand out of my bed and touch Joe by the shoulder in his bed. We complained and cursed together. We accepted the rough tour conditions all the way to the end. At the end of each performance I respected the load-out, because I respected my bandmate. Its highly disrespectful to expect your bandmate to bare the burden of loading all the band-gear. It is courteous to help with all the gear not just your own. Do not be the musician that packs their instrument without helping with the rest of the gear. Approach the job like a hired mover, use a dolly and get to work. Do not rush the process because whatever you are rushing the moving job for can wait. When I am playing locally I am responsible for loading my own gear. I pack my drums in my car first, then get paid afterwards. It is an unwritten rule in the music world; play locally and load your own stuff. If you play on the road you help the band. When I am ready to be paid, I walk over to the band leader and ask, "Are you ready to settle up?" That is my way of asking for my money. For some reason that is the least awkward way for me to ask. I heard the late Chico Banks say that to Lindsay Alexander, a Chicago Blues artist, after a gig at the old southside, "Checker Board Lounge" and I have been using it ever since. It sounds respectful yet direct. Most importantly I feel comfortable saying it. Next, I will discuss the perils of alcohol use after a show.

When the last note is played and the crowd is losing their minds, you probably want to celebrate. That feeling is normal. I cannot tell you how many times I have been offered a drink from a fan during and after my set. I really wish they would have put that money in the tip jar. But the reality is, they would rather have an experience with you. A few minutes of conversation with shots and beer will make a fan's day. They want to ask about your music influences, songwriting, gear, and etc. However, you do not need a drink to socialize. It is easy to abuse alcohol night after night because it is a good time, and it is mostly free to the band. When I toured with the Shawn Kellerman band I went straight to the bar right after the last note of the set. After a drink or 3 I signed a few cd's and disassembled my kit. Next, I helped packing the van. Then I went back to the bar until they closed. Joe, our bassist was sober for at least 10 years, and he put up with my drunken buffoonery almost every night. He never belittled me about my drinking. I think a social drink after a show is ok. If you can handle it. The problem is the social habits become a lifestyle because of nightly repetition. I encourage every touring musician to break up your road habits. If you drank last night, then go sober tonight. Do not fall into the trap of drug abuse and alcoholism. Take the time after the show to sell some merchandise, meet some fans, and take advantage of the opportunities that may be in the room. If you are looking for a fresh opportunity on the road, chances are you are not going to get it being drunk after the gig. If you were a record executive looking for a new act, would you invest in a drunken musician? If you are sober at the merchandise table, back-stage, venue lobby and parking lot then you are approachable. Whoever is interested in your art may be watching you in all those places.

Now at this point, the van is packed and you have the option to retire to your room. However there may be an after-party. I will discuss some ways to take advantage of a great opportunity for career advancement.

In the Blues world there are parties that take place after festivals at local bars, clubs, or hotel ballrooms called *jams*. Most Blues fans encourage the musicians to drink excessively at these events. As soon as you walk through the door, fans applaud you, and offer you a drink. Fans have surrounded me with shots, free beer, weed, and whatever regional drug available. My early years on the road I thought this was the greatest thing ever. I was getting all this attention, free party favors, and the opportunity to jam with pro musicians. I have had some fun nights doing this, but the problem was my playing was sloppy, because I was drunk. When you play at jams, fans often record the performances and upload them to YouTube. It is not good for your image to be on any virtual platform drunk. Another reason to remain sober at an afterparty is networking. Some artist may attend parties looking to replace a band member. Others may be looking for extra musicians to record their upcoming projects. If they were considering you after your 9 pm festival performance, they will pass on you after your 2 am drunkenness. When these kind of mistakes are made, the good times make them easy to repeat. Nobody is going to tell you that you are blowing your opportunities. You will never know how many of them you missed. You will wonder why less skilled musicians will keep moving up the success ladder while you stay in the same place. Your conduct is just as important as your skill. No band-leader wants a liability. If you cannot handle your drinking at an after-party, why would a person want to hire you? The correct thing to do at an after-party is network soberly.

If you are employed by an artist, you must know the gig is not going to last forever. The more contacts you have the better when you become unemployed. If you formed good relationships with other bands, as soon as your gig is over you can make an easy transition to the next band. Make the after-party hang work for you. Shake hands and meet some new people. Take a selfie with people you want to form relationships with. Give them a follow-up call a few days later and send the selfie pic to them so they can remember you. This really helps to break the ice on a first-time call basis. I often engage with people at parties, and sometimes they forget me. But, when I send them the selfie, they remember me. When I first started making follow up calls I was nervous. It felt awkward contacting strangers. I had to get over my shyness. I learned that we all can use a friend in the small world of the music business. You never know when a band needs a substitute musician and they are performing in your town. If your picture and contact info is in their recent call log, most likely you are going to get the gig. When I make follow up calls I just say, "*Hello I am just calling to see how you are do-*

ing. It was great meeting you at the party the other night." If they do not remember me, I send them the selfie. Now that I have discussed the importance of sobriety, I must give you a warning. You may quit drinking and realize you are the only sober person in the band.

When I quit drinking alcohol, I had to adjust to being around drunk bandmates. Suddenly the shoe was on the other foot. I learned that alcohol and band business do not mix. Which brings me to the next rule. Never discuss music business with a bandleader when they are drunk.

Artist may have post-show celebration drinks which inspires false aspirations. The artist may request more rehearsals, and songwriting sessions, demanding the band must play better or record more songs. Only to forget about it the next day. My problem was listening, and believing these drunken artists. I was the band member holding on to every word they slurred, only to realize 12 hours later it was the alcohol talking. Presently, when I hear a drunken rant from an artist, I just nod my head and smile with deaf ears. Because, the real meetings happen when all parties are sober. I also learned to be careful when you discuss music performances with drunken musicians.

Alcohol and serious thoughts do not mix. Most musicians are serious and emotional about music. Every artist is sensitive about their musical abilities also. Some hide it better than others. I have witnessed drunken debates amongst band members that start in a harmless discussion but then someone talks about a sour note someone played, and the finger pointing starts. Before you know it, all hell breaks loose. It is important to critique your bandmates in a sober rehearsal, not at an after-party.

In the next chapter I will illustrate, how I pack for a flight. I will also share some stories about flying that supports a simple rule, *"Do not Freak Out."* When you fly, situations happen beyond our control, but no matter what, you must remain calm. I have ridden in tour buses and vans. I will discuss proper ways to travel in both.

CHAPTER 8

Don't Freak Out While Traveling; Airplanes, Tour Busses, and Vans

Travel light as possible when you fly. Luggage weighing over 50 pounds is considered too heavy and you may be charged an extra fee by the airlines if your bag is over the limit. I condense my luggage to one carry-on bag and one suitcase for checked baggage. I keep at least two pair of underwear, socks, t-shirts, 1 stage out-fit, toiletries, and 1 pair of drum sticks in my carry-on bag. This is important because, if your suitcase is lost, you still have stage clothes and your instrument with you, in case you must go directly to the gig upon arrival to your destination.

Take a picture of your luggage and your passport before you leave home because a photo helps identify it, if it gets lost. In this case, a picture is worth a thousand words. Next, I will cover what to do when things spiral out of control. The rule is simple, *Don't Freak Out.*

On June 1, 2009, I was touring Europe with the Bernard Allison Band. We had a flight scheduled from Paris to Frankfurt Germany and we were waiting at the gate, in the Paris-Charles Gaulle Airport. While we were watching the TV monitors, "Breaking News" abruptly reported, Air France flight 447 crashed over the Atlantic Ocean. After the announcement, a few would-be passengers, startled by the news began exiting the boarding area. Flight attendants rushed to turn off the TV monitors. I looked at our bassist Jassen, and Bernard, they were cool as cucumbers. Bernard figured, "If they already had a crash today, what's the chances of another one?" We boarded the flight and the flight went smooth, until it was time to land. The pilot made his usual landing announcements in French and German. When the wheels touched down the plane violently bounced down the run-way. The overhead compartments flung open, and passengers screamed in French. I was yelling a few last words in English as well, I thought we were crashing and going to die. The plane bounced about seven times and settled. Traditionally when a pilot makes a smooth landing outside of the United States the passengers applaud the captain, well there was only crying this time. We deplaned to smoking runway tires, ambulances, and firetrucks. This was my first official plane crash but it wouldn't be my last. I was scared as hell, but I didn't *freak out*, I got off the plane and I kept my cool.

In 2010, I was with the Blues Band Mississippi Heat, we were flying into Budapest Hungary. It had been a long trip and I wore gym shoes on the flight. The last 30min of the flight I took my shoes off as the plane was descending. I must admit my feet smelled bad. I noticed it and before I could put my shoe back on, the guy next to me said some unfriendly Hungarian words (I'm pretty sure it was profanity) and used his hand to cover his nose.

I was embarrassed so I apologized, put my shoes back on, and tied them up. A few minutes later the plane was touching down on the runway. I was sitting in isle seat, as he was in the middle seat to the left. The plane had slowed down, but still taxing down the runway when the man unbuckled his seatbelt and rose out of his seat. He violently stomped my ankles and feet with his hard-bottomed shoes, while forcing his way into the aisle, which hurt immensely. Once he stumbled over me, he opened the over-head compartment, grabbed his bag and stood facing the cockpit. I finally took off my seat-belt, stood in a crotched position, and upbraided him. It took great restraint not to punch him in the back of the head. As he stood with his back to me, his nonchalant attitude angered me, as if I was no threat to him. When we deplaned I wanted revenge but, reality set in when I saw soldiers patrolling the immigration check-point. When you enter a foreign country, they have a line for visitors and separate line for locals, and the local line was moving swiftly. When we got to baggage claim my assailant had gathered his bags and was gone. I wanted to tell the bandleader Pierre about the attack, but he was busy filling out lost and found forms for Carl Weathersby's Gibson 335 guitar, which was lost during the flight. Carl a veteran Blues guitar player had the sweetest sounding Gibson ever, and the airlines misplaced it. My assault by an angry Hungarian wasn't more important than the lead guitar player not having his prize guitar. We were starting a tour and I knew what happened to me on that flight, was where it was going to stay. I didn't bother mentioning it to Pierre. I knew that if I had run down my foe in the airport, it would have resulted in a trip to a foreign jail so, I had to be cool about it, and yep you guessed it, I didn't freak out, although I sure wanted too. Another example of me holding my composure during times of stress was in 2013 touring with the Shawn Kellerman band, featuring Lucky Peterson.

Lucky Peterson (R.I.P. Lucky Peterson, b.12-13-64, d. 5-17-20) was a legendary bluesman. He hired us to play with him in Moscow, Russia. The gig was great, it paid a $1000, we played the second largest venue in Russia, and stayed in a 5-star hotel. The flight back however, was a nightmare. About 3hrs in, all the screens in the head rest suddenly turned off. The interior lights went out and the emergency lights along the floor of the aisle turned on. The plane was dimly lit. The captain spoke over the intercom in Russian. I knew it was serious when, the passenger next to me started crying and rubbing her hands across her chest and forehead in a catholic style, air-crucifix motion. About a minute after the first announcement a second pilot spoke in English, "This is the pilot speaking, we have lost electricity on the plane and we are losing altitude, we are having some complications, please remain seated." I had a window seat right above the wing and I could see half of it shifting back and fourth, as if it was struggling to extract. I could feel and hear the grinding of metal underneath my feet. I realized the pilots were trying to land the plane. The Russian aviator made another announcement and this time the lady next to me went ballistic. I'm thinking, what could he say to upset this lady further than she already was? Then they shared the English version of bad news, "Sorry folks this is the captain again and we are going to have an emergency landing, we are having some trouble with the landing gear, everyone must remain seated." I looked out the window and I could see the wing shifting, grinding back and forth, harder and harder. I realized the captain was trying to get the wheels out for the landing, but the generator wasn't producing enough power. I leaned forward and saw my friend Joe, he was in the same row a few seats over. We locked eyes, I smiled and I gave him the *rock on* hand signal, thumb, index, and pinky finger erected. I was content with the idea of dying on a plane ride back from Moscow. I thought if I was going to go, this is the way to do it. I just rocked Moscow! I felt I would become a "Blues Martyr." I crouched out of my seat to visually check on Lucky whom was seated two rows up. To my surprise he and his wife Tamela had blankets over their heads, asleep. I figured if I was going to die I would want somebody to wake me, so I could settle my affairs with God. I took off my seatbelt, staggered over the crying catholic woman and, walked to Lucky's aisle seat. I took his blanket of his head and shook him awoke. I said, *hey man the plane is going down*. He looked up, shrugged his shoulders and said, "O.k.". He put the covers right back over his head. I figured he didn't understand due to being sleep so I said, *No man, we about to fucking crash!* He moaned something that sounded like, "O.k., O.k." and he put the blanket back over his head and that was it. Talk about keeping your cool, Lucky was the coolest, he didn't even bother to wake up his wife. I went back to my seat and started praying hard because at this point I could see tree tops as we gained speed on our descent. After a little while the wheels of the plane detracted, and the trees departed. We had a rough landing on an abandoned airstrip outside of Stockholm, Sweden. When we deplaned, the wheels of the jet was smoking, ambulance and firetrucks were approaching the scene. City busses came and picked us up and took us to an airport, which was quite a distance from the abandoned airfield, were we landed. We arrived at the airport and were separated according to country of origin. All the Americans were offered a nearby motel room, and a meal while the Russians were detained in a room at the airport overnight. The next morning, we were driven back to the airport for a 6am flight. I could have fainted when I realized they were bussing us back to the same abandoned airstrip, to board the same plane that previously failed. I was paired with the same crying catholic woman and she wasn't short on prayers on the ride back. She cried and prayed all the way to the United States. I kept my cool on the outward, inside I was a wreck, I didn't *freak out* but I think I would have been excused if I did. Flying isn't all bad, most experiences are great. It's the quickest means for short trips, but longer tours may require a bus. Fortunately, my bus experiences felt much safer.

Throughout my time in the Bernard Allison Group we travelled Europe on a tour bus. Bernard was affiliated with a German tour agency, "Touronado." I felt like a rock star, stepping off the plane, and onto a bus. I love the sleep I get on a tour bus, the hum of the engine and rocking motion is relaxing. The first time I boarded the bus and claimed my bunk, Bernard explained to me, "Don't sleep with your head toward the front of the bus, if the driver slams the breaks, you can snap your neck." I slept with my feet towards the driver every tour.

We couldn't defecate on the bus, and there were no showers so, hotels nights were a relief. It's a horrible feeling to wake up on a cold January night discovering you must "#2". You must alert the driver and hold it until he drives to the nearest rest stop. After a big plate of foreign food this may be highly uncomfortable. I learned to stay away from rich stews and anything with peanut sauce on a bus night. Another discomfort on tour busses is the lack of privacy.

If you share a tour bus, you live in close quarters. Private phone conversations are heard, snoring, and sick germs are easily spread. It's common that if one band member gets sick, by the end of the week the whole band including the driver is sick. It's a good idea to keep hand sanitizer with you, and wash your hands as often as possible. Now that I've covered tour bus living quarters I will discuss handling laundry duties on the road.

Tours last longer than your clean laundry will so, I suggest you pack a small bottle of detergent to hand wash your underwear. I also use hotel hand soap as a substitute. You can hang small amounts of laundry on your bus bunk curtain to dry. Tour buses are a comfortable way to travel. It allows the band to sleep horizontal, which is a luxury in comparison to traveling in a van. I will share some experiences and lessons I learned touring in them.

Out of all the years I've played music professionally I've spent the bulk of my time in vans. I've lapped the U.S and Europe rolling in vans full of band gear, with Ana Popovic, Mississippi Heat, Bernard Allison, Shawn Kellerman, Liz Mandville Greeson, James Armstrong, Anthony Gomes, and many more. When you are invited on a tour be sure to ask about the means of travel and if you are expected to help drive. Some bands share in the driving responsibilities while others don't, some even hire drivers. Driving on tour is a serious responsibility and you want to be well rested beforehand. If you are not, driving could be hazardous.

In 2016, my friend James Armstrong invited me to play drums on a tour thru the Mid-West. James left his Springfield Illinois home at 7am and picked me up in Bloomington Illinois around 8am. We drove two and a half hrs to pickup his son James Jr, whom had flown in from Norway. James Jr landed at Chicago O'hare International airport just minutes before we arrived. The father and son hadn't seen each other in some time and it was a joyous reunion. We drove to the first gig which was an hour or so north of Madison, Wisconsin. After the long drive we got to the club, unloaded our gear and had sound check. We rehearsed a few songs and ate some dinner. We changed into our stage clothes in the bar restroom and played a hell of a show. James plays Blues with a lot of emotion, he really gives the audience everything he's got. After our 30min set-break we played another 60min set. After the show, the band packed the van, I was extremely tired but we had an hour ride to the hotel. We got in the van and hit the highway. The band was talking about the gig and we were all buzzing from the standing ovation we received. Well, the excitement wore off as the hum of the tires grew steady and soothing. After about 20min or so, our exhaustion kicked in and the van was totally silent. James was driving, and I knew he was sleepy, he kept rubbing his face and yawning. He turned on MPR or CNN radio, his favorite broadcast. I was sitting shotgun and I felt the responsibility to keep James awoke after our long day, so I talked to him. I grew tired, it was after 2:30a.m. and my eyes were starting to exhaust. I fell asleep and minutes later, I woke up with my face pointed toward the window, when I noticed we were extremely close to an 18-wheeler truck. James was drifting into the right lane. I looked left and James was fast asleep, the whole band was. I could hear snoring over the radio. We were maintaining speed and moving closer to the truck by the second. I wanted to wake James, but I didn't want to startle him, so I lightly touched his shoulder. He pulled his head forward and clutched the wheel. James lightly steered back into the left lane while exclaiming, "I'm awake boss." "Boss," is James term of endearment for his close friends. I didn't alert James to how close we came to a wreck, instead I turned the radio to the late night hip-hop station, woke up the band, and rolled down my window for fresh air. I talked to the band and cranked the jams all the way to the hotel. We were fortunate we made it safe but other bands aren't so lucky.

Lil Dave Thompson was a Mississippi Blues artist I met in January 2010 at the Kingston Mines. His band sounded great and on his set break his drummer invited me to sit-in. Asking guest musicians to sit-in is common practice at the Mines. I played a few songs and at the end of the night Lil Dave and I talked. Dave told me he liked my playing and his drummer couldn't make the upcoming tour dates. Dave asked me to sub the tour and, if it works out, become a permanent member in the band. He told me the dates but, I was already booked. On February 14, 2010, Dave was driving late after a gig on the aforementioned tour and fell asleep at the wheel. As a result, Dave died from a van accident, his band members survived but were severely injured. I felt horrible this happened. I could have been in that van. I think of this and many other situations when it comes to driving after a gig. It's important to be well rested before you drive, it's never a good idea to drive sleepy. Along with being well rested comes the responsibility of traveling safe with band gear, I will discuss the rule for that too.

Packing band gear correctly is very important while traveling. If the gear is packed higher than the back-seat you must have a barrier to protect the passengers. I've been in vans where if the driver presses the breaks, the instruments start rolling forward. This is dangerous, especially at high speeds. If a keyboard stand is loosely packed on top of drums and luggage, a slam on the breaks could result in it hitting someone in the back of the head. If you own a van for touring, make the investment of getting a cage or wall installed in the back of the van for safety. If the van is a rental don't pack the gear higher than the back seat, unless you have a temporary barrier to install. Michael Dotson is a Chicago Blues guitarist for Mississippi Heat. While on tour Michael always rides shotgun. He never gets in the backseat of a tour van, I noticed and asked why. He told me stories of musicians that died on the road from car accidents when he played with Magic Slim. He said, "The ones in the backseat died from the gear, not the collision."

In the next chapter, I will highlight a part of the music business that may seem uncomfortable, which is negotiations. I will share experiences throughout my career where I had to negotiate pay for live gigs and recordings.

CHAPTER 9

Negotiations, What Are You Worth?

My first touring Blues gig with Liz Greeson and the Blue Points in 2003, I didn't negotiate because I wasn't good at playing Blues. When I played jazz with Chris Green and New Perspective I was referred by my mentor Vic Jackson. My goal was to impress him so, I never thought about money at all. By May 2014, I had been playing professionally for 11 years, and I was starting to understand my worth. I arranged with Kelley's Hunts manager Al, to fly me out of Bloomington Illinois to our gigs. Once he started doing this it became a standard part of my negotiations with every touring band afterward. It was an 11 year stretch of touring before I realized my worth, and I next I will explain how I negotiate.

When I get a call for a gig nowadays I know exactly what to ask for, but this confidence and knowledge came over time. When an artist manager calls, it can be very direct and cold. I'm comfortable with this and I continue to be myself no matter the tier of the artist. I don't create a phone persona when I'm handling business, I'm direct and honest. I ask if an artist is signed to a label and tour agency. If so, I know the artist can afford to pay well. Next, I ask if the artist wants to hire me for a *tour,* or a few *spot dates?* Spot dates are just a few shows typically over a weekend, tours last longer than a week. Spot dates are out of town and they should pay more that local gigs. If you are flying to spot dates, then you know the artist can afford to pay handsomely. If you are riding in a van or, driving yourself to spot dates, you may earn less depending on the artist and venue. I have earned anywhere between $400-$1500 for a spot-date and $400 per show for tours. If a job is offered under my rate, I inform the caller my rate is firm because, it's what I charge the other artist I currently work with. Since its well known that I work with established artist they get the picture and pay my asking price. If they refuse to pay my rate, I don't do the job. Next, I will discuss tour Ryders.

Some recording artist offer individual tour riders for the band members. A tour rider is a clause in the band contract that gives each artist whatever they need backstage before and after a performance. This could be anywhere from a personal masseuse (if you're a top-selling artist) to a plate of food. Alert the tour manager about the items you want in your Ryder. I ask for sparkling water, soda, candy, snacks, fresh fruit, and coffee with honey and cream.

When I'm negotiating for a tour or spot dates I ask about hotels, and I negotiate my own room. I ask if the band is staying at someones house while on the road. Some bands may want you to stay in a fans house instead of a hotel. It can be a nice experience but, sometimes it's uncomfortable. I don't stay at the bands fans or, friends houses anymore and here's why.

I was on tour with the Kelley Hunt Band in 2015. The manager asked the band to stay at a "friends" house. I didn't want too but I figured I would help save money. We pulled up to the house and it was beautiful. We greeted the home owner, settled in, and he invited us to the backyard for a BBQ. After exchanging pleasantries he poured some drinks and I detected he had a few before we got there. In between flipping pork chops the host ask if I was hungry. I said *sure*, and I asked, *Do you have anything other than pork?* The guy replied, "Hey man you're not a Muslim, are you?" I'm not Muslim, but the way he asked was bigoted. I felt this familiar tension with bigoted fans and I've always dealt with it circuitously. I answered the host, *No, I just don't eat pork*. I excused myself and went to the bathroom. After I urinated, I was angered when I discovered President Barack Obama toilet paper. I had never seen that before, I didn't even know Obama toilet paper was ever manufactured. I was disgusted at this point, but I kept my cool. I couldn't freak out because I had already agreed to stay at the house and, I knew the artist had already planned to save the $100 it would have cost for a motel room. I was thinking, never again.

Be sure to ask if you are staying with fans, or friends of the band, before you go on tour so, you can negotiate for a nightly hotel. Don't wait till you are in a bad situation to demand a hotel room. Some clubs own houses known as band-houses, specifically for touring bands. Some are clean, while others unkept. If you are staying in a band-house or Air B&B, bring your own towels and toiletries. Another aspect of negotiations involves tips.

When you play bars and clubs a tip bucket is sometimes placed on the bandstand. If the vocalist is great and the band is tight, the tip jar could be over flowing. This could mean an extra $50 or so added to your base pay. Some bandleaders don't share the tips with the band, they may decide to keep them to cover tour expenses, while other bands split the tips evenly. Don't assume the tips are going to be shared with you, ask in negotiations. If you confront the artist after the gig about the tips it can be an awkward conversation resulting in your last gig with the artist. Artist may not handle confrontation well, in fact money isn't publicly discussed in some cultures, so it's better handled over the phone prior the tour.

Never ask for a raise, this is a recipe for disaster. When you negotiate salary for a gig you must realize, whatever you negotiate for, will be permanent. Raises are rare in the music business. If you desire more money, take on more responsibilities for the artist. You can sell merchandise on set breaks, write songs for the artist, drive the van, or act as a road manager. Making yourself more valuable is a way to earn extra money without asking for it, because if you ask for a raise, most likely you are going to be fired. Another important part of negotiations involves pay for studio work.

When I negotiate for studio sessions I have a typical price if, I don't personally know the artist. If the artist is signed to a label and they have a budget I ask for $200 a song. If it's an hourly rate I ask for scale which is $350 for 3 hrs. Demo work pays a little less, I ask for $100 a song if its local, and I may settle for $50 if

I want to establish a relationship with artist. Taking less money and doing a great job on a recording can result in you playing future gigs with the artist, this rule extends to church's too, as mentioned in the introduction. Some churches have small budgets when they record so its o.k. to bend a little. When I record for my friends I don't charge anything. I like to use the barter system. I play on their projects and they play on mine. I negotiate gas money and lunch otherwise.

When you become a veteran musician never take a low paying job, unless you are financially desperate. Low paying recording sessions can be the biggest headaches. They are typically given by new, or insecure artist. If the artist is new, they may be nervous about the session. This can result in long unpaid rehearsals. A new artist in the recording booth can be a nightmare or a heavenly dream. You won't know until you invest your time. If the session pays by the hour, its o.k. to sit around waiting for the artist to get their act together. If you are getting paid per-song you don't want to spend endless hours in the studio. You want a smooth flowing session. The insecure or under-prepared veteran artist are the worst. They've recorded many albums but still waste valuable studio time. If the session pays by the hour who cares, more money for you. If it's a per-song basis then try not to pull your hair out, be patient, and give your best performance. Negotiations can be handled many ways and it should change throughout your career. The higher your skill level, and the gigs you are offered on a steady basis, will determine your price. Food is a part of negotiation as well.

Most tours offer one square meal per day. I generally ask for this because some tours offer per diem and not food at all. This doesn't require negotiation, it's just good to ask. Some per diem may be as high as $100 a day while some is just $20. When I play locally I don't receive per diem and I rarely ask for food unless, I'm playing a wedding reception or restaurant.

Wedding receptions typically pay $175-$300. You want to ask for food because the food looks awesome at receptions and it's a long day. Don't assume you are going to eat the Beef Wellington the guest is served. You may be in the hotel kitchen eating a turkey sandwich with chips, but at least you won't go hungry.

Negotiations are used to leverage more perks and money on your gigs, but what do you do with the money? In the following chapter I will share with you some of the financial mistakes I've made and how I corrected them.

CHAPTER 10

Be Smart With Your Money

One thing I wish I would have done throughout my career is save my money. I spent tour money on frivolous things. I bought cheap jewelry, fast food, alcohol, and lots of marijuana. All the cheap jewelry I bought either broke or faded, and the rest was bad for my health. When the tours were over I went home, payed my bills, partied with my friends, only to be broke all over again. Honestly, I didn't care, I felt successful because I was touring. This went on until I had my daughter. Becoming a parent made me realize I must be disciplined with my spending. I learned to use my money to support my family. Also, I had to put some money aside for a rainy day, because after the tours are over the bills keep coming. You may get fired or the bandleader may decide to take a break from the road. If this happens, you will be forced to live on your savings, if you were smart enough to put some away. One piece of advice I have for musicians is, don't spend your money at the venue you perform.

I was watching the movie, *Hustlers* starring Jennifer Lopez. Lopez's character was a New York City exotic dancer whom drugged and stole money from her clients. There was a scene in the movie where Lopez scolded her co-worker because she used her own money to buy a drink at the bar. She asked, "Are you investing in this place? Well, if you're not, then why are you buying drinks, let the clients do that, spend their money, not yours." This also reminds me of what my friend Kenny Coleman a veteran Chicago drummer once said to me, "If the promotor didn't buy it, it ain't in the diet." These two pieces of advice serves me well. J-Lo's character was right and so was my friend Kenny. When you earn money at an establishment you shouldn't give it back to them, you are not an investor. If you want a drink let a fan or promotor buy you one. If no one offers you a drink, then don't drink at all, save your money. Before I followed this advice, I drank at bars and clubs all over Chicago, right after the downbeat of my last song. I went straight to the bar and purchased a cognac. I paid for it in hangovers and late-fees, which added to my late bills. If you don't purchase things you don't need, you will have more money for things you do, like music equipment.

I've seen musicians perform with cheap crappy gear, while drinking. I can't believe the condition some musicians that call themselves pro's, will allow their gear to be in. I've seen drummers with cracked cymbals, guitar and harmonica players with buzzing amps, and bass players with old muddy strings that needed changing. You must keep your gear in top shape. This rule is important for every musician, no-matter the tier of the player. If I get a squeak in my drum hardware, a cracked cymbal, or a dent in a drum-head, I address it immediately. I do this because, if I get a call to go to the studio for a recording session my gear is ready. I may not have time to go to the instrument store to replace a drum-head or cymbal. Also, when you perform live you want to have your gear in top shape so, other musicians respect you. I pay attention to the condition of musicians gear and I judge accordingly. If you play unkept instruments, it shows you don't care about your craft. Who wants to hire a musician that lets their gear go to the dumps? Even if a veteran musician is using inexpensive gear, I still expect it to be in top working order and tuned as best as possible. We all can't afford the most expensive drums and amps but we all can have pride in the way we look and sound. Investing in your gear is investing in yourself. If you are in the stage of your career where you can't afford the most expensive instruments that's o.k., just take care of what you have. If you are a drummer, purchase drum cases for your drums. If you can't afford cases, plastic storage bins (preferable with wheels), retired golf bags, and large duffle bags work just as well. Cases help regulate the temperature of an instrument and, protect them from the rain, so they are highly important.

Two of the last purchased items became the most valued of all my drum gear. I encourage every drummer to purchase a quality drum throne with a backrest, and a cart. My fiancé bought me a throne with a backrest and my playing changed immensely. I was able to practice more comfortably because my lower back finally had some relief, resulting in longer practice time. I wish I would have purchased one long ago. Another purchase proving valuable is my cart. Every working drummer should have a moving cart with wheels or, a dolly. It saves trips and time when you are loading into a venue. Another great way to invest in yourself is pursue your dreams. If you are a side-musician and you want to start a band or solo career, then save your money and buy some studio time or home recording equipment.

I know musicians that have amazing talent. They can write songs and sing. If you are at the stage of your career where you have artistic endeavors, then don't wait for the opportunity to come fall in your lap. It's going to take some money and effort. Crowd funding works, and so does your own 2 cents. So, be sure to cut out the bad habits that may be holding you back. If you spend money on fast food, cut the fast food your waist-line will thank you. Buying your food at grocery stores and planning your meals is cheaper than eating on the run. Put the money towards fulfilling your dreams.

When I toured in the past, I spent a small fortune on gas station snacks, I still get a sweet tooth on-tour but I'm mindful of my spending. Those little gas stations stops really add up. I learned to pack some snacks from home in my bag, and take advantage of the free hotel breakfast if possible. They normally have fruit, granola bars, muffins and nuts that can get you through the day till dinner. I also take some of the back-stage catering with me after gigs, this comes in handy for the late-night hunger pains. All of these decisions I make may seem impractical but the savings are worth it. The money saved can be used to fund projects, to further express my artistic creativity.

Another investment that is very important to me is my health. I encourage every musician to get a gym membership or develop a home exercise routine. When I drank excessively I wasted a lot of money. I bought a fifth of cognac and a 12 pack of beer at least 3 times a week. I spent about $30 a bottle and another $15 on the beer. That's about $130 weekly on alcohol not including what I spent when I went out with my friends. I was overweight, and I was developing gout in my right foot from the combination of late-night greasy food and alcohol. I woke up with the worst hang-overs and limped to the restroom on my sore foot. I had the "shakes" too. I knew my drinking had to stop because it was getting in the way of the music. It was changing me for the worse.

In 2013, I was playing drums with Chicago Blues Artist Wayne Baker Brooks. We were the temporary house band for ABC's "Windy City Live" morning television show. I had to be in the studio at 7 a.m. for load in, and we taped at 9 a.m. The night before one of the tapings I couldn't sleep. I decided to have a drink to "settle my nerves." I had a cognac and beer. One round turned to several. I got drunk and passed out. My fiancé woke me at 5:00 a.m. and asked, "Hey babe, are you on TV today?" That's when I grabbed my head, sat up in the bed and exclaimed, Oh shit! I wiped away my tears, as my career flashed before my eyes. Here I was, a drummer with a TV gig and I wasn't responsible. I was drunk, and could barely walk. I had to be at work in 2 hours and it was a 2 and half hour drive to the TV station. I was a wreck, there was no way I could make the drive from Bloomington Illinois to Chicago that fast, and that drunk. My fiancé was incredible that morning. She got me dressed, made me coffee, and drove me to work at 90mph. Dawn is a professor at Illinois State University and she had to be back in Bloomington for a 11:00 a.m. lecture. I fell asleep on the drive to Chicago and woke up to a screaming headache. We made it to the television studio at 7 a.m. I couldn't believe she drove me to Chicago and made it back for her lecture. If it wasn't for her I would have lost a job on TV, which was an incredible opportunity for me. I think about the risk I took, and the mistakes I made due to drinking. I encourage every musician with an alcohol problem to seek help. You must spend the money you earn wisely. I spent $130 per week on drinking and a YMCA membership only cost $70 a month for my whole family, that's only $17.50 a week. When I compare that to the $130 plus, I know I'm in the right direction. I'm more productive in life, because I wake up without hangovers. I use my mornings wisely instead of sleeping well into the day. I look and feel better because I frequent the gym. I'm productive in my song writing because I have the extra money for studio time. I'm a better provider because, I buy groceries for my family instead of alcohol. All of these realizations came with maturity, and discipline, which gave me a different focus on life. In my career I learned that you must be responsible in all things. In the next chapter I will discuss, the importance of logging gigs in calendars, paying taxes and child-support, and why they shouldn't be ignored.

CHAPTER 11

Scheduling Gigs, Paying Taxes, and Child-Support

It's very important to keep a log of your gigs on a calendar. When I get a call for a gig, I look at my calendar before I accept it to make sure I'm not already booked. If I'm open for the date I mark it in my calendar immediately. A record of your dates also illustrates how many shows you play annually, I currently average about 100-150.

When you file your taxes, you can deduct mileage and food purchased while on the gig. Also, you can deduct stage-clothes, hair products, hair appointments, cosmetics, ride sharing cost to and from gigs, airplane baggage cost, auto-insurance, car repair, car tires, musical instruments, instrument repair, file sharing cost, music streaming services, website cost, cleaning bill for stage clothes, stage shoes, parking for gigs, travel tolls to and from gigs, phone data storage, and accounting cost for taxes . When you receive a 1099 from an artist, it's important to log them, and pay your taxes. You can't be taxed by an artist unless you earn at least $600 performing with them in the, State of Illinois.

Another rule for musicians is pay your child support. If let your child support payments accumulate over $2,500 the state of Illinois can revoke your license and suspend your passport. If you don't have a drivers license, you aren't considered dependable which could hurt your chance of getting gigs.

Passports are the second thing to go if you don't pay your child support. If you don't have a passport you will miss out on the best tours music has to offer. For the Blues world, cruises and international touring is the most lucrative. To maximize your career, you must play internationally. I have been fortunate to have travelled all over the world playing Blues. In fact, the most money I've made on tour has always been overseas. If I wouldn't have paid my child support, I would have missed the beautiful experiences traveling provides. Next, I will share a rule for social behavior amongst musicians.

Chapter 12: "Mind Your Business"

When you play locally, it's easy to get caught up in the gossip of the music scene. Who's dating who, who's cheating, who stole who's gig, and so on. The Chicago Blues scene can host a nightly soap opera and I avoid being a cast member. There is constant gossip about relationship failures, band drama, and whatever else that goes along with booze after 2 a.m. I've learned to avoid the negativity. When I see musicians arguing I walk away, instead of walking toward the confusion. When I hear musicians bragging about their sexual conquest with the club employees, or fans, I never chime in. I don't have any stories about sleeping around on the Chicago Blues scene because I don't do it. I don't hold court with musicians that are there for the booze and meaningless affairs. Instead, I converse with the players that are trying to get ahead in their careers. I ask about who's making a record, or what artist is embarking on a tour, not who's sleeping with whom. When I see an artist making bad choices like, using hard drugs or having sex in the restroom stall at the local Blues club, I don't talk about it. I don't gossip to other musicians about what I saw. I pretend like I didn't see anything. If you gossip, you never know if the person committing the moral offense will find out its you that's spreading the news. If the person denies what you saw, it could make you out to be a liar. Either way it won't fall in your favor. You don't want the label of being "messy." This advice applies for touring musicians as well.

You never know a musician until you travel with them. The nice easy-going musician can be a wild party animal on the road. In my early years I travelled throughout the United States extensively. I shared rooms with band members on most tours. The guitar player in one of my former bands is highly respected on the Chicago Blues scene. He's an older gentleman, he must have been 60yrs old when we toured together, and he dressed like a church deacon. He wore wool sweaters and white collar shirts, with black orthopedic shoes. When he talked he rarely used curse words. I thought I knew him until one night after an early gig in Tampa Fla, I decided to go out. There was a popular strip of bars near our Motel 6 called, "Ybor." I left, and the guitarist decided to stay back at the motel and "get some rest." I had a few drinks and after an hour or so, I went back to the motel. To my surprise I walked in the room and the guitarist was receiving a blow job from a hooker, while smoking a crack pipe. He was so high when I walked in the room, he didn't even notice I was there. I was standing in the room with my bottom jaw hanging in utter disbelief. The hooker never stopped giving head under a cloud of smoke, she didn't even acknowledge my existence, and the lights were on. I didn't even know this guy smoked crack, let alone partied with hookers. When I got over the initial shock, I walked out the room and closed the door quietly. I went back to Ybor and had some more drinks. I waited till the bars closed and went back to the room. When I got back to the motel, my roommate was snoring like a buzz saw. The next morning, he asked "How was the bars?" I said, they were o.k. I wanted to poke some fun at him, I almost said, not as much fun as the hookers and crack, but I didn't. I was wondering if he saw me in the room while he was partying, but I could tell from his demeanor he had no idea I was there. I just told him, I had a good time and left it at that. I didn't want to embarrass him. I never mentioned what I saw to him or anyone. After that tour I never looked at him the same. I mentally lost respect for him but he doesn't know it. He's recommended me for sessions and gigs over the years and I figured, if I would have gossiped about him and disrespected him I wouldn't have had those opportunities. So, I encourage every musician, no matter what you see on the road, don't gossip, just mind your business. Another rule I will discuss is, never ask a musician about the company they keep.

One of my bandmates was always with a woman, I assumed was his wife. He brought her to almost all his local gigs. One day she wasn't with him, he had another woman on his arm. I pulled him to the side after I saw them snuggling and kissing. I asked him, *Where did you find the sidepiece? Shouldn't you be careful with the public displays of affection?* He looked at me annoyed and whispered, "I'm here with my wife, the other woman you see me with all the time is my girlfriend." I had to pick up my jaw quickly, and I could tell by his demeanor I had overstepped my boundaries. I never asked him or another musician again who they're with. Another rule of minding your business involves salary.

Before you accept a gig, you have the right to negotiate your pay. You must realize that your pay maybe more or less than your band mates. Avoid discussing pay with band members if you are asked to-do-so by the bandleader, artist or manager. When you are asked not to reveal your salary to anyone else, most likely you are earning a different amount than they are. If you get paid separately from the rest of the band, or you are not an original member of an established act, you may receive unequal pay. I only talk about pay with the musicians I have worked with for many years, they are my friends. I know that we receive equal pay because we work in the same capacity. In these circumstances it's ok. For example; I've been working on the Chicago Blues scene for over 20 years, I know what the venues pay. I can discuss the pay with my local musician friends because we all know what to expect. I know the conversation isn't awkward or meant to be a big secret. However, if I'm on a tour I don't discuss pay. If pay is discussed and I discover I'm earning less money than my co-workers, I don't complain or quit the gig over it. The higher paid musician may sell the band merchandise, write songs for the band, drive, or tour manage. Whatever the reason for them earning more money is none of my business. Now that I've covered respecting your co-workers boundaries, next, I will discuss respecting ourselves, which involves self-discipline.

CHAPTER 12

Respect Yourself

Never give musicians anything to talk about other than positivity when it concerns you. Positivity spreads slowly while negativity spreads like wild fire. You can play on a killer album and it will take social media posts, streaming thumbnails, hired publicist, and gossip before your friends and peers find out it exist. However, if one of my friends have a fight in a club parking lot, get caught with their pants down in a bar stall, or whatever embarrassing situation you can imagine, I will hear the news within 24hrs. To develop a good reputation you must, be on-time for every gig, play great, and keep your nose clean, literally. It takes 5 minutes or even 5 seconds to destroy a good reputation that it takes a lifetime to build.

I had developed a reputation of drinking and partying on the road in my early years. Dave Herrero was the only Chicago artist to fill me in on what was being said about me. I was considered a liability. The word had gotten out that I was a great local drummer, but I was a party animal on the road. Chicago artist stopped calling me for road gigs. I didn't even realize my reputation was soiled. I decided to change that. I stopped getting wasted on the road, and I stopped public intoxication. I knew that alcohol was the source of my problems. The musician's that was on the road with me was gossiping about my crazy road antics. I didn't know that my road habits where causing me to be a joke on the Blues scene. I decided that I had to change by not giving them anything to talk about, other than positivity. Respecting yourself also involves respecting others around you so, the next rule is highly important.

Never attempt to sleep with anybody's spouse on the music scene. This was a harsh rule to learn because, I was on the flip side of the coin for this one. I never tried to approach anyone's spouse in that way, but a few musicians have tried to approach mine.

I was playing a show with a Blues artist in Kansas, City. I brought my fiancé with me and we drove separate from the band. During the show, the artist wanted me to play a drum solo. While I was giving my best Dennis Chambers impersonation, one of the musicians left the stage and went over to my fiancé table and sat beside her. I didn't know what he was saying to her, but my fiancé seemed uncomfortable. Turns out he was propositioning her right in front of me. After the show, I sat at the bar with the band and we talked about the show. I was just getting to know the band and I wanted to spend a little time hanging out with them. After a little while my fiancé and I decided we were going to the motel and we said our goodbyes. We got to the car and she told me what happened while I was on-stage. I was crushed, and to make matters worse I had to play 2 more gigs with the band. The gigs were awkward, but we handled it well. My fiancé and I both agreed that we wouldn't say anything. It took great restraint not to confront the musician. I thought about telling the bandleader, but I knew it would put him in an awkward position, what was he going to do, fire the guy mid-tour? Well, it turns out I would have to suppress this feeling for some time because he's a Chicago musician and, over the years we have worked on various projects. If I would have confronted him, we never would have worked together. We have performed international tours, recorded albums together, and this book is the first time I ever mentioned it. I've decided to forgive him, but I don't recommend him for gigs because, I can't vouch for his character. I don't know if he will treat somebody else's partner the same way he treated mine. I really appreciate my fiancé for taking the high road on this matter. She could have confronted him but, since the advances stopped she didn't. I love her for that and so many other reasons.

When I decided to play with the Kelley Hunt band in 2014, Kelley wanted to meet my fiancé. It was a big deal for her to meet the partners of her band members. She tells the musicians in her band, "If you are married or soon to be, there will be no cheating in my band, If you are single you can do what you want." I respected Kelley for this and I understood her position. She knows it's wrong for musicians to cheat on their spouses and she refuses to be complicit in the matter. She's the only artist I've ever worked for that has this rule. When you are married the musical community knows it. They watch every move you make. If an artist meets you and your spouse on one gig, and see you with your "side-piece" on another, this may cause the artist to lose respect for you resulting in you being fired.

    I know an artist who had to fire his drummer for cheating. The artist and his wife was at a state fair enjoying his day off when she spotted his drummer, whom was married, with a woman that wasn't his wife. The artist wife confronted the drummer on the spot. The drummer tried to deny being on a date, but it was too late, she saw them holding hands. The wife of the artist was upset because she was friends with the drummer's wife. She wanted to know if her husband (the artist) knew the drummer was having an affair, how long had the affair been going on, and did he have any girlfriends as well? The artist had to fire the drummer upon his wife's request, so he called me to replace him. I couldn't believe I had scored a great touring gig because the drummer was a cheater. His loss was my gain. If you are single and ready to mingle, you still must be careful about sleeping around because, some people are just plain crazy.

    I was on-tour with a band and we were in Kansas City, Mo. We played a gig and the bass player met a woman. She was attractive, in her mid 50's, divorced, and active on the dating scene. The bassist went home with her, and the next day bragged to me and the keyboardist about the fun he had. About a week later we were in Buffalo New York, and the woman showed up about 30min before showtime. She flew halfway across the country to see my friend with no warning, she just popped up. When she walked in I recognized her immediately. I greeted her with a big hug and smirk on my face then, I directed her backstage and followed her, so I could see the look on my friends face when she exclaimed, "Surprise." My friends jaw hit the floor, his one-night stand from last week had followed him 981 miles. I could have been a better friend and warned him she was in the venue, but I just couldn't pass up the comedy. He could have sunk thru the floor when she greeted him. She was excited to see him, she talked extensively about her flight and, how she missed him. Some minutes later we took the stage, I was laughing inside, and my buddy had the blues, literally. He didn't want to look in her direction, so he nervously tuned his bass and tweaked his bass pedals in between songs. She stood in front of him, shimmying her chest, and cheering loudly all night. During his bass solo she put her fingers in her mouth and whistled as loud as she could. When the band leader announced his name, she screamed at the top of her lungs to let the others ladies in the room know that he's all hers. On the last note of the set my buddy stormed off-stage and made a dash to the dressing room. He told us and security not to let her in. He didn't leave the dressing room to sign autographs or anything, he was waiting for her to leave. Needless to say the woman was crushed, I saw her face as she watched the door of our dressing room swing open and close, without him coming out. She got the message and left. At the end of the night we had to pack the gear. We went out to the parking lot and saw the van in disbelief. The jilted groupie used red lipstick and wrote a long letter to the bass player on the windshield. She literally had to hold her 50 plus year-old body, on the hood of an 18-passenger van, to write in small caps about how she felt disrespected and, mistreated. I still wonder to this day if she used a step-ladder, it was creepy. The bandleader wasn't happy to say the least, and my buddy could have crawled under a rock. The soap in the car wash wasn't strong enough to remove the wax-based lip stick without extensive elbow grease. The rest of the tour the bass player couldn't live it down, we talked about it endlessly and my jokes rubbed it in. Every show on the remainder of that tour he looked over his shoulder wondering if he had a stalker. Another rule I will discuss is, don't illegally hustle at the gig.

    The Chicago blues scene can be a big party. Blues lovers come from all over the world looking for a good time. Fans like to drink and some like to do drugs. Some musicians sell drugs at the gigs to make some extra cash. Selling coke, weed, and whatever else can bring home a handsome profit at the end of the night. This may seem like a good idea, some of my friends make a living doing this, but I'm completely against it. I've never told another musician not to sell drugs, I figured they wouldn't listen. Selling drugs is not for me because I value my career. I can't afford lawyers to fight a cocaine charge and I don't want to go to jail. I don't want people to think of me as a drug dealer, I want to be known as the best Blues drummer in Chicago. When people mention my name all I want attached to it is musicianship. I want to get calls for gigs, not weed. Also, selling drugs takes a lot of time and focus away from your craft. Looking for a source to buy drugs can be a time consuming task and hoping nobody "rats you out" can keep you up at night. Traveling to and from gigs with drugs in your car can get you sent to prison. All it takes is a traffic stop and all your hard work and practice is in vein. Some musicians spend their whole career selling a little something on the side and, they never get caught. Some get caught and you never hear from them again. I don't need extra cash that bad. The music has been taking care of me just fine. If I feel the need to earn more money I just practice and play more gigs. I can sell my own t-shirts, autographed drum sticks, music, and this book. I don't want to be apart of anything that can take away from my brand. Think of yourself as a corporation like, Coca-Cola. Everything they sell is an extension of their brand, which is soft-drinks. They sell vitamin water, tea, energy drinks and the like. When you think of Coke you think soda, when you think about Andrew Blaze Thomas I want you to think music, which directs us to marketing.

In 2016, I was playing a gig with Nigel Mack and the Blues Attack in Indianapolis Indiana at the Slippery Noodle. At the end of the night, Blues Music Award Winner Biscuit Miller and I had a talk. Biscuit is good friend of mine and he asked, "Why don't you have your name on your bass drum? Blaze, you play so good, people should know who you are, just like James Knowles used to do." James Knowles died in 2014 and he was one of Chicago's greatest drummers. I never thought of myself as an elite talent, like James. I realized, if I don't think highly of myself then nobody will. When I returned home my daughter and I went to the art supply store and bought glitter, stencils, and paint. I bought a new bass drum head and we painted my name, we added glitter and had a fun time making our art project together. Since I've added the new bass drum head to my kit I noticed more traffic to my website. There is a famous story about one of my favorite drummers, Bernard "Pretty" Purdie. Bernard is a legendary drummer. When he recorded for Steely Dan, he had a sign on his drum kit that read, "You have hired the world's greatest drummer." I think that's the coolest thing ever. Most musicians would never be bold enough to proclaim something like that. Bernard did it in the 1970s and we talk about it in the present day. I decided after that conversation with Biscuit that I need to brand myself. I needed my own proclamation.

After touring with Ana Popovic band, I went on to play in other bands. I ran into her backstage at a festival some years later and we caught up. She told me out of all the drummers she worked with, I was her favorite. Boom, that's where my proclamation came from. I made a voicemail message on my phone stating; *this is your favorite drummer Andrew Blaze Thomas, I can't come to the phone right now because, I'm either in the practice room, recording studio, or on-stage, please leave a message and I will get back to you at my earliest convenience.* Sometime later I was playing a gig with the James Armstrong band. When James announced me on-stage he told the audience of my voicemail, calling myself, your favorite drummer. He made some funny statements about it and the audience cracked-up. James can be very funny and witty on-stage. When he did that, and I saw the reaction from the audience, I knew I was on to something. I added that statement to my website, my Home page writes, *Your Favorite Drummer.* My confidence grew over time with that statement, and it all came to fruition when I played with "Monster" Mike Welch in 2019, at the Tampa Bay Blues festival. In front of an audience of over 10,000 Mike announced me as, "Your favorite drummer, Andrew Blaze Thomas." I was using my iPhone to film the gig for my YouTube channel and I use that intro from Mike on my videos. I know there are many drummers that came before me. I'm aware that I'm not everyone's favorite anything. There are many legendary drummers and they all played great, but none of them called themselves, *Your Favorite Drummer*. I'm happy to say that's all mine!

Social media can be a great tool for self-promotion, but you must be careful. When I was on Facebook (prior to 2019) I posted tour pictures. I wanted everyone to think that I was successful. I took selfies on the biggest festival stages, television show sets, theaters, big recording studios, and exotic locations boarding planes. I fell into the trap of mentally competing with my peers. I wanted the illusion that my life was perfect. I didn't take pictures of the small bars, restaurants, and home studios I still worked out of. I didn't share what it was really like to be me. Every gig I play isn't a big production, but I wanted everyone to think I was on top of the world. I became jealous of other musicians when I wasn't working. I saw what my peers were posting, and I thought, how did this person get the gig I'm better than them, or why is this musician on the road and I'm at home? I didn't realize I was jealous of musicians acquiring gigs that weren't meant for me to have. I was being envious. I was posting pics for likes and positive comments. If somebody gave a negative comment or even said a joke about me on social media I couldn't take it, I would block and unfollow them. I was letting social media affect the way I looked at my career. I had to realize that I didn't need social media to be successful. I was already touring and recording records with Blues legends before social media became popular. Facebook didn't make my career. I've never had a gig offered to me that was worth my time on social media. Every gig I ever had I earned through playing, networking, and nurturing relationships, face-to-face, not virtually. When I realized this,

I took a break from social media. Now that my head and ego is in the right place I'm back on social media to promote this book, and future projects.

I was talking with my drum student, Skyler From a few nights ago outside of Kingston Mines Blues club. He told me he contacted a band on social media and landed an audition. I was blown away that the world has changed. When I started my career, I went to music stores and looked on the "musicians wanted" particle boards and called bands for auditions. I went to jams and got skipped over on *sign-in sheets* (a list of names in numerical order of musicians waiting to participate in a open-mic jam) only to play last to an empty room. I went to drummers gigs to met their bandleader, to break the ice in hopes of one day being a sub. I replied to the Illinois Entertainer and Craig's list drummer-wanted ads, and prayed. It was a faith based, full-time gig, looking for a gig and I couldn't believe my student landed his first major audition, on his lap-top, go figure. I have shared rules developed to keep a gig, but every side-musician gets fired even if you follow a set of rules more strict that mine. As my friend and veteran bassist Ari Sedar said, "You're really not in the music business until you get fired." In the next chapter, I will discuss the statement no side-musician wants to hear, "Musically, I think I'm going to go in a different direction."

CHAPTER 13

How To Handle Getting Fired

I jokingly call my mentor Tony Braunagel, the hardest working drummer in show business. I'm impressed by his resume, he's had some amazing gigs. Tony was on-tour with Robert Cray in 2009, and I caught up with him on the road. He invited me on Robert's tour bus. He was excited, they were touring in support of a new record entitled, "This Time," and Tony had played masterfully on the record. While talking about the bands upcoming tour dates, he explained he had a problem. He opened a copy of a popular Blues magazine, flipped to the middle and on the left was an advertisement of Robert Cray at an upcoming festival, on the right was an ad of Bonnie Raitt, playing a different festival on the same day. Tony had been Bonnie Raitt's drummer for several years and was still in her band, while working with Robert. I thought this is the coolest problem ever. Two of the top-selling Blues acts in the world both wanted him on the same day. I asked what he was going to do? He was in a pickle, which do you choose? He obviously loved both artists. He established relationships with both of them. I thought to myself, I want a problem like this one day.

In 2011, I toured with the Anthony Gomes band and we started working on Anthony's upcoming album, "Up 2 Zero." We were in St. Louis recording some demo tracks and my portion of the session went well. A week went by and Anthony hadn't sent me any tracks. I asked him about it on the road and he told me the bassist was still over-dubbing some parts and, they are mixing it. The following week we completed a weekend of spot-dates, we all hugged and said our goodbyes before heading home. We were off from Sunday to Friday, and then we were going to start a tour throughout the Southwest. Thursday of that week Anthony called, and I thought he wanted to talk about the setlist for the up-coming tour. After about a minute of small talk, he dropped an atom bomb in my lap. He said the words no side-musician wants to hear, "Musically, I think I'm going in another direction." I was driving at the time of the call and I had to pull off the highway to avoid an accident. I couldn't believe what I was hearing, I was stunned, it was my first time getting fired. I had just moved in with my fiancé, I agreed to pay half the rent and I was suddenly unemployed. I wasn't playing with any other bands at the time. I had invested all my time and energy into supporting Anthony's dream. When I recovered from the initial shock, I said, *Anthony, thanks for the opportunity to play in your band*

and, if you ever need me in the future for anything please don't hesitate to call. I mean it o.k. He assured me he would, and we said our goodbyes. I thought about the conversation we had on the side of I-55 north for several minutes. I was upset and confused, I didn't know why I was fired. Was it something I said, the way I behaved, or was it my playing? I wanted to call him back and ask but my pride wouldn't let me. I thought about the record, "Up to Zero." I was so excited to be a part of his next album and suddenly it was all over. I was so invested in Anthony that, I was out of the local loop. I was out of the Chicago scene for a while because I moved to Bloomington, Illinois. I wasn't networking anymore, I wasn't hustling, I became complacent. I was comfortable just being Anthony's drummer. I had a rude awakening and, I had to get back to the grind. I learned to never become complacent, don't ever just play with one artist. If the artist dies, get sick, has a baby, decides to quit, or fire you, what are you going to do? I couldn't blame Anthony for being out of work, I had to blame myself, for not working with another artist while working with Anthony. I should have maintained relationships and kept playing locally in between tours with Anthony, just in case something like this happened. After about a week, I went back to where it all started for me in the Blues world, "Big Rays Jam." I cut my teeth and scored my first road, and local gig at that jam. I had to go back and let my peers know, I was looking for work. I made the 2 and half hour drive to Chicago from Bloomington several times a week jamming and networking. It took 3 months before my phone rang regularly. During that time my practice became razor sharp, my focus was renewed.

When I look back at that time I'm grateful Anthony Gomes fired me. It gave me a better understanding of the business, thicker skin, and sharpened my focus. It made me a better business man and musician. A few years later Anthony played a show at the Castle theater in Bloomington, a few blocks from my house. I went to see him and we talked after the show. I told him he sounded great and the new rhythm section was impressive. I was comfortable around him and the time we spent was genuine, we both didn't have any hard feelings. It was burning my tongue to ask him why he fired me, but my pride wouldn't let me. I decided it wasn't important. Sometime after our reunion Anthony called me for a string of dates, but I was already booked. That's when I realized I was on the right path because, he fired me then tried to rehire me. This happened because I didn't harbor any ill feelings toward Anthony. I maintained a professional attitude, and told him, if he ever needed me don't hesitate to call. This statement is helpful, when you get fired because, it sets up a future working relationship. I am fortunate to call Anthony Gomes my friend, we call each other a few times a year to catch up. I call him every time he releases a new album to say congratulations.

When I was fired by Anthony I didn't see it coming. Some years later I was fired again but this time I was fully aware and, it worked out in my favor.

In 2017, I was alternating tours with the Kelley Hunt Band, and Billy Branch and the Sons of Blues. I was also playing locally with Nigel Mack and the Blues Attack, Grammy Award winner Billy Flynn, and James Armstrong. I was able to keep it all going smooth until Kelley and Billy's schedules overlapped. I felt just like Tony Braunagel a few years prior, I had a good problem. Kelley had a string of dates throughout the summer, and Billy had the Chicago Blues fest main stage booked, a string of international dates, and he was ready to record an album. I wrote a song for Billy's upcoming record and we were regularly performing it live. Billy wanted to play my song on the Chicago Blues fest, the largest Blues fest in the world. I was in a pickle, I loved Kelley's music, she is one of the best singer-song writers out of Kansas. I didn't want to quit her band, it was a sweet gig. I talked to Kelley's manager Al on the phone to explain the situation and he wasn't having it. Al at this point, had established a no subbing-out-the-gig policy in Kelley's band. I wanted to play the Chicago Blues fest and maintain my gig with Kelley. I understood his position, Kelley deserved a consistent band she could depend on and, her manager didn't want a revolving drum chair. I knew Al was annoyed with my call when, he told me abruptly, he would call me back in a little while. I knew then I was getting fired. A few minutes had gone by and I got a call from Rick King, a veteran Chicago Blues drummer. Rick asked, "Are you still working with Kelley Hunt? I just got offered the gig from her manager." I wasn't surprised, I explained the situation to Rick, that I had the Chicago Blues Festival booked with Billy. Rick could relate to the situation very well, he's a few years older than me so, he had been thru this situation lots of times. He told me that he was accepting the gig, but he wanted to be sure he wasn't over stepping boundaries. A few minutes after I hung up with Rick, Al called me with the, "I think we are going in a different musical direction speech." I thanked him for the opportunity and, I told him if he ever need me in the future for anything, don't hesitate to call, and I meant it. I respect Rick King for calling me, he didn't owe me that. He called to check on me, he also wanted to know, what kind of situation was he was entering. I learned from Rick that if you know a musician personally and, you are offered their gig, give them a curtesy call. It eliminates awkwardness and ill feelings. Also, the courtesy call can help guide your decision on whether you want the gig. If it's a messy situation, you may not want it. I also learned, be careful accepting gigs that you can't sub out. There may be times you want to work with other artist and you can't because, if you sub out the gig you will be fired. Ask during negotiations if the manager is o.k. with you subbing out the gig from time to time. If it's not permitted, be sure you love the music, the gig pays well, and the dates are plentiful. When I was fired by Kelley's manager, it wasn't an impact like the Anthony Gomes firing. This time I was well diversified, I was playing in multiple bands, and I had a new career in song-writing. I got to play my song, "Call Your Bluff" for an audience of 20,000 plus at the 2017 Chicago Blues Festival. When you are diversified, getting fired isn't a bad situation, it just makes room in your schedule for more opportunities. In the next chapter, I will discuss the pitfalls of spreading yourself too thin and, the impact it can have on your reputation.

CHAPTER 14

Don't Be The "Jack Of All Trades", Before You Are the Master Of One

With the completion of this book I will be a professional drummer, song-writer, YouTube creator, educator, and author. Drumming opened the door for all the other jobs I have. When I started writing songs, I realized I had an advantage over the average writer. I had relationships built with recording artists through drumming. I figured, since I had some songs written, I could pass them on to the artist I was already working with. However, for these artists to take my songs seriously, I had to be an outstanding drummer.

I was on the road with my friend, Blues recording artist James Armstrong. James was looking for a permanent bass player in his band. He hired a young musician from St. Louis to go on some spot dates that would serve for his audition. When I met the bassist, he was excited to tell me about all his gigs back in St. Louis. He talked about rappers, and indie-rock artists he played with. He had a job blogging for a website, and he talked about being a sound engineer. He even offered to record and mix some of my demo projects. We talked about all of this within the first hour of our van ride together. On the way to the gig I was thinking, man for this guy to be so young he must be an amazing talent. When I was his age, my focus was solely on drumming. I didn't think to branch out to so many career endeavors. We got to the venue early so, James wanted to rehearse. James Armstrong is very particular about his music. He's a great songwriter and his show isn't the gig where you can just mail it in, if you don't study James songs you will be exposed right away. I knew the rehearsal was going to be really good or, really bad when the bass player didn't have any notes. If a musician plays a new gig without notes superbly, then you know they have a great memory. James asked the bass player, "Where's your notes?" before we started playing and, he gestured to his temple and said, "I got it all up here." We started song one, which was the simplest of the set-list and the bassist wasn't good at all. In fact, he was horrible. His amp was too small and that's unacceptable in the Blues world. If you listen to James record's, you will notice he likes his bass tone big and fat. The bassist brought a small amp because he said, "It was convenient." Besides his sound being all wrong he didn't know the songs. When James asked if he knew the arrangements, he replied, "I didn't have time to study, I just listened to them a little because, I was busy with my other stuff." At this point James was frustrated but, I was hot as a fire cracker. I was ready to choke this guy, I was thinking, the nerve of him to get on stage with a world-class Blues band without doing your best to prepare. I calmed down after the fruitless rehearsal and pulled him aside for a talk. I asked why he wasn't prepared. I was ready for the uncomfortable conversation because I just had to know what he was thinking. James was a recording artist, with a calendar full of tour dates and, he was giving this guy a chance to become a touring musician. We had come from two different worlds and I just couldn't understand it. If I was in his position, there's no way I would have arrived to a gig under prepared. The bassist talked about his girlfriend, personal problems, and all the other jobs he had. When it came to James music, he listened to the songs a few times and showed up. After the mini-tour I never saw or heard of the guy again. He missed out on a great opportunity with James. Even if he decided not to take the gig full time, he still could have had a good relationship with me and the rest of the band. I probably would have taken him up on his recording and mixing offer, but I figured if he lacks the discipline to study for a gig why would I hire him to work for me. One job would extend itself to another if you perform the original job masterfully. Robert Green is the author of, "Mastery." He stated, in order to master a craft, 10,000 hours of practice time must be applied. I suggest all musicians must employ the 10,000-hour rule. That's about ten years of focused practice. When I completed my ten years of study, my other jobs came naturally. I was ready to become all the things I am today because, I was a drummer first. Spreading yourself too thin is a mistake when your original craft isn't mastered but, what happens when you are sufficient in your craft? What if you are focused solely on one job, which is performance? Is it still possible to take on more than you can handle? I will address this in the next rule.

"Don't bite off more than you can chew" when booking gigs. This rule is personal, it's not for every musician. Some musicians thrive on the challenge of playing multiple new gigs at a time, but I learned it's not for me. When I work with an artist for the first time I want to make a good impression. I want to play their music flawlessly. I realized 3 new gigs in a week is pushing it. A setlist from an artist may have 15 or more songs. On a 3 set show, that's a total of 45 songs. Some of the songs usually are covers I already know, but songs become confusing when there are 20 songs with the word, *Love*, in the title. Having good notes help, but I want to make every artist I play with feel comfortable. If I'm spreading myself too thin, I don't play my best and every artist deserves the best out of me. If I have 3 gigs with 3 new artists, the rest of the gigs that week must be with artist I've already played with. The only way to find that limit is through failure, but once you find your limit stick to it, unless you are financially desperate. If you are in a financial bind, make the best notes you can, play the gigs the best you can, and enjoy being in demand. Having too much work is a great problem to have! Next, I will share the importance of reading books.

CHAPTER 15

Read Books For Enlightenment

Reading, helped my development as an artist, I will share some of my favorite books. *The Big Gig; Big-Picture Thinking for Success*, by Zoro is an amazing book. Zoro explains how to succeed in the music business through his experience of drumming with the top R&B acts. Zoro's book is faith-based and highly motivational.

Amir "?uestlove" Thompson's, *Mo Metta Blues*, is an inspirational masterpiece for all musicians. He shares his experiences of drumming in his band, "The Roots," producing for Grammy winner D'Angelo, and presently drumming on NBC's, "The Tonight Show with Jimmy Fallon."

Mike Levine's, *How to be a Working Musician* serves as my "Bible" for the music business. I use it as a reference for contract negotiations, manager obligations, gig salary ranges, and more.

Sheila E.'s, *The Beat of my own Drum*, is a powerful memoir. She revealed how she overcame depression from being raped as a child, touring the world with *Prince*, and becoming one of the world's top selling Pop artist.

Hill Harper's, *The Wealth Cure,* is a great book even though Harper isn't a musician, he's an actor. I purchased the book because, I thought it was about, how to earn more money. It turns out, he shares how to make better choices with the money you already make. This book changed my perspective on my finances.

Robert Green's, "Mastery" is a collection of narratives from accomplished inventors, scientist and artist that elucidates how they achieved their career goals thru 10,000 hrs of focused study, or practice time.

Mark Binelli's, *Screamin' Jay Hawkins All-Time Greatest Hits*, is inspirational. Jay Hawkins has an amazing story of challenges he faced being a black man in the music industry, during the *Jim Crow* era. Jim Crow was a term used for white supremacy segregation laws that was infringed upon blacks in the southern United States.

Buddy Guy's, *When I Left Home* is a great book. I perform at, "Buddy Guy's Legends" club several times a year. Buddy tells the story of the struggles he endured to get where he is today. Buddy was a part of the post WWII Northern migration of blacks to Chicago and he is a major influence for modern Blues. These books motivate me because the people in them overcame hardships and became successful. Zoro, Amir "?uestlove" Thompson, Sheila E., and Hill Harper, shared their daily routines that prevents complacency. Next, I will do the same.

CHAPTER 16

Avoid Complacency; Always Search For The "Next"

It's easy to get lazy in the music business when you have a steady gig. When you receive a touring schedule covering the next six months to a year, you may get comfortable with the money and tour life. You may stop looking for new sounds, new technology, and new ways of expressing yourself musically. You're playing may become robotic. Sure, you may play your steady gig well, but have you lost your ability to create on the fly? Do you still have your chops? Can you step out of your comfort zone? If you are a touring Jazz musician, have you been to a Blues club lately? If you play Blues, when was the last time you went to a jam and, sat in with some serious fusion players? You should take the time to study new techniques, and music while you have a steady gig. When you get comfortable, you may stop listening to the up-and-coming musicians, which can result in sounding dated and predictable.

When I study new music I play along with songs in my streaming library, and I go out to jams and sit in with musicians I don't know. I do this, so I don't lose my chops. I watch the up-and-coming drummers play solos with their lightning fast licks and innovative chops on Youtube, it inspires me to practice. I like to have that hunger, that little voice in my head driving me to play better. I don't desire to play fast anymore, I just want to play better.

I must avoid complacency by having order and structure in my day. I wake up around 9 a.m. but this varies depending on if I had a gig the night before. When I get up I make coffee and watch 30 minutes of Sports Center and then the news. I keep it to 30 minutes because the sports news runs on a cycle. 30 minutes is all I need to catch up on my favorite team. If there are no catastrophes in the world I turn off CNN and go to my practice room. I practice drumming for 90 minutes and take a break, then practice for another 60 minutes. I complete the second half of practice and go to the gym. After my workout I go home and shower. Next, If I don't have any lessons to teach, I decide if I want to write a song, make a YouTube video, or finish writing this book. I teach lessons or write around 1 p.m. When the doorbell rings and it's my student or writing partner I am ready to work. I like doing all these things because I am making these things happen on my terms. I am making the phone calls, setting up the sessions, and putting in the work. Nobody is asking me to do any of this, I do it because it is an outlet to express my creativity. I use my social media platforms to create as well.

My digital platforms are YouTube, Facebook, LinkedIn and my website, andrewblazethomas.com I use these to display my talents, achievements, and teach. I didn't realize I would have so much knowledge to share with the world before I started my channel. My practice room doubles as my YouTube studio. I have over 400 subscribers now and someday it will be in the thousands. I watch "how to" videos to learn how to grow my channel. It is a new job for me, I feel successful every time I gain a subscriber, it is all a part of the journey.

After my early afternoon work is done I spend time with my family. We eat dinner and sometimes I watch a movie, play a board game or play video games with my kids. I love being a family man.

Having a daily schedule is something that you can control, but there are some things in the music business that you can't. In the next chapter, I will discuss how to cope with loss. I will share my advice on how to handle losing a bandmate, to being fired and my experience in losing a band-leader to death.

CHAPTER 17

What Happens When You Lose A Band Member?

What happens when your bandmate gets fired? What if you are close friends, should you warn your friend if you know they are going to be fired? Unfortunately, during your career there may be situations like this which are beyond your control.

Grammy award winning producer Michael Freeman says, "When a band member gets fired it's like losing a family member." I agree with Michael and, it's worse when you know your bandmate is getting fired, but they don't realize it. Sometimes a band meeting is held by the manager to alert the band there will be a replacement, with auditions. Warning your friend of their firing may lead to a nasty confrontation between them and the band-leader, resulting in you losing your gig too. Then what about dealing with the new musician in the band? Are you disloyal if you befriend them? There is no straight answer other than, be professional as possible. Try not to get in the middle of it, and do your job the best you can so you are not fired. Next, I will discuss losing a band member to death.

In August 2018, I began touring with Welch-Ledbetter Connection. Mike Ledbetter was one of the greatest Blues singers of the last decade. Before every show Mike warmed up his operatic trained voice backstage. He practiced his various scales and breathing techniques as he paced in circles. His stage-presence was outstanding, Mike danced, cued the band, and even dropped down to his knees on his encore ballad every performance. "Monster" Mike Welch was the guitarist and his playing is regarded as on of the best on the scene today. He's a good songwriter too. The rest of the band was Blues Music Award winner Scot Sutherland on bass, Luca Kiella on B-3 organ, and myself as the drummer. This was one of the most talented Blues bands I ever played with. We never held rehearsals, we just played, and it was great from the first note. We toured Russia, Europe, and played some spot dates throughout the States. Mike Ledbetter and I became friends. Ledbetter had his own solo Chicago Blues band that I played in as well. The scheduling was perfect, we toured internationally as the Welch-Ledbetter Connection and when we returned home to the Chicago Blues clubs Ledbetter had his solo dates lined-up. I was still balancing my gigs with Billy Branch and the Sons of Blues, and a few other artists.

On January 21, 2019, I was in Santa Fe, New Mexico recording an album with a Blues artist, Michael Bloom, when Mike

Ledbetter called. I took a break from the session to talk to him about our future music plans. Our tour agent booked us on the 2019 Legendary Blues Cruise, an east-coast recording session, and festival dates throughout the summer. We were excited about making a new record. Mike sent me the demo songs and they were great. He told me he was having a backyard birthday party for his 1 year old son the upcoming weekend and invited me. I told him I would see him Saturday and we said our good-byes. After our talk, I joined Michael Bloom in the studio and we finished recording for the day. On the ride back to Bloom's house from the studio I received a disturbing call from our tour manager reporting Michael Ledbetter died from a fall sustained from a seizure in the shower. I knew Mike suffered from epilepsy, but I couldn't believe it. I was hurt, I couldn't believe he was gone. I asked Bloom to pull over to the side of the road, I needed a moment to process what I just heard. I got out of the car, cried, and screamed for several minutes. I didn't care about the touring opportunities and potential record deals. I would give all those things away just to hang out with him again. The memorial gigs we had in his honor was special. Musicians I hadn't seen in a long time came to pay respects and collect money for the family. The Blues Cruise wasn't the same without him. Welch-Ledbetter Connection won a 2019 Blues Music Award for Band of the Year. I couldn't have been prouder to be in that special band. Mike was only 33 years old. That taught me a lot about life and music. Life is not promised to us so, put your heart in your music, play every show like it's your last, and appreciate your bandmates. Ironically, Mike Ledbetter's last show was where my Blues career started, B.L.U.E.S on Halsted. In the next chapter, I will share my experiences, philosophies, and opinions on race and how it effects the life of a Blues musician.

CHAPTER 18

Race And The Blues

As I'm writing it's July 2020, and the world has changed due to the murder of George Floyd on May 25. George Floyd was an unarmed Black man, killed by a Minneapolis police officer. The officer arrested Floyd because he was accused of purchasing cigarettes with a fake $20 bill in a nearby corner store. The confrontation turned violent when officer Derek Chauvin placed Floyd in handcuffs, pinned him face down, and chocked him with a knee on his neck for over eight minutes which resulted in his death. Onlookers recorded the broad-daylight murder on their cell phones, and it was broadcasted to international news outlets causing a world-wide outrage. His murder was called, "A Modern Day Lynching" by members of Congress. Floyd's murder caused racial tensions to erupt. Many people were distraught by it and used their social media platforms to denounce white supremacy. However, some whites used their platforms to support the police and to discredit the "myth" of state crime, and institutionalized racism. White Blues fans who I thought were my friends, displayed their support of the police by posting "Blue Lives Matter" emblems, and "George Floyd was not a martyr," slogans (a phrase coined by a black female socialite Candace Owens) on their Facebook pages. I had no idea that some of these white "Blues fans" felt this way. I thought, what if I was George Floyd? Would they think I deserved to be killed by police because I passed off a fake $20? The Blues scene is dominated by white fans, artists, record label owners, club owners, and music marketing outlets. Of these white artist and "Blues supporters," some are empathetic and knowledgeable about the historical struggles of blacks and they express it in songs. Then there's the white "Blues fans" and artist whom are not knowledgeable and frankly don't care about the plight of African-Americans. Shame-fully African-American Blues artist shy away from denouncing white supremacy, or state violence in fear of offending their white fanbase and support system. Because, of the money white "Blues fans" spend, and ownership power they possess, the experiences I will share in this chapter is commonplace for Black musicians but rarely publicly expressed. I will share three stories from the road which has helped me form this rule; *be aware of your surroundings*. This includes people you consider fans, and places you visit on your tour routes.

In 2003, I was on the road with Liz Greeson and the Blue Points. We played a bar gig in north-western Indiana, that was a familiar routing date for Liz but, it was my first time there. We played a pretty good show so, after the gig I went to the bar and started flirting with a woman. We engaged in conversation when suddenly, bassist Dave K grabbed me off my bar stool and whisked me into the van with no explanation. I was dismayed and confused by his behavior, I talked to women after gigs prior and he never acted this way. On the drive back to Chicago we talked about it and, unbeknownst to me Dave K was looking out for my best interest. Dave and Liz told me we were amongst Ku Klux Klan members and I was flirting with one of their girlfriends. I knew it was a biker-bar but, I was ignorant of the danger I was in. Liz warned me, "The next time we are in a place like that, I should be more careful." As I look back on it now, I never thought to ask the question, *why we were in "a place like that" anyway?* However, her advice would prove valuable throughout my career because, unfortunately there are many Blues shows throughout the United States held in "places like that." And, to add insult to injury, I was given a warning by Liz on my behavior, even though the ones who basked in bigotry and hate was completely tolerated. I learned that white supremacy organizations are alive and well and I must be aware of them. I have to be aware that just because people may be "fans" of the music that doesn't erase the hatred in their hearts. As the old saying applies, "They want our rhythm but not our blues."

In 2005, I was on tour throughout Europe with Bernard Allison. We pulled up to a hotel in Dresden, Germany and, before we got off the bus Dave Brown, out tour manager gave me a short speech. Dave warned not to wonder off alone in Germany and, if I left the hotel, take a band member with me. I asked why, and Dave exclaimed, "Skin heads attack people on the street here." I took the warning with a grain of salt and went out by myself for daytime errands and after-hour bar hopping. Later in the tour the band had a travel day. We took a train into Burn Switzerland. We got off the train, walked toward the exit and saw a group of eight skin-heads playing a game of Hacky-Sack(a soccer like game using a small soft ball). They looked like extras from the 1979 cult classic, "The Warriors." They wore mohawk or bald-haircuts, eyeliner, nose-rings, torn dingy flannel shirts, skinny jeans with torn knees, dangling dog chains, and Doc Martin boots. When we walked past they stopped playing Hacky-Sack and stared at us with grim faces, I stared back. After that moment, I obeyed Dave's orders of staying in groups for the rest of the tour. I was reminded that white supremacy hate groups are not exclusive to the U.S, they are world-wide.

In 2009, I toured with the Shawn Kellerman band. Shawn is a white Blues guitarist, Joseph Veloz is a Mexican-American bassist and myself an African-American drummer. The fact that we were all different races playing Blues made an interesting dynamic, but we didn't think about it until we played majority white towns.

Bowling Green, Kentucky, was one of those towns that made you think about race as soon as you arrived. Confederate flags are displayed proudly on license plates, bumper stickers, and roadside billboards. Shawn booked us a gig at bar, and after we set up our gear, Joe and I hung out on the patio. A white bar patron, no doubt a local of Bowling Green asked what was Joe and I doing there, in a southern drawl. This question wasn't foreign to us, we knew his meaning as to say, *What are you two nonwhites doing here in this majority white bar.* Joe informed the bold man we where members of the band. He asked us, "Do you guys feel comfortable?" in a very sarcastic tone. The truth was, we both didn't feel comfortable but, Joe and I wouldn't give him the pleasure of our thoughts. Joe said, "Of course, why wouldn't we be, we're here to entertain you." After the man had a sense we weren't intimidated he went into the bar. Being confronted by the Bowling Green bigot, and my experiences with the formentioned bands was a reminder, that when you are a person of color on the road, you must be aware of your surroundings. Your survival depends on it. I was fortunate not to have been attacked in any of those situations, but drinking and flirting with Klan members girlfriends, navigating European streets under the gaze of Nazis, or playing small towns where Confederate and American flags coexist, just isn't smart. Now that I have shared some experiences concerning race and traveling, I want to share a lesson I learned through meeting another Black musician.

In 2014, I met an African-American bassist from Nashville named Justin Henry. It was understood that Justin was a temporary hire for the Kelley Hunt band. Justin was talented and eager to work with us. Our first few hours together was a bit awkward. Justin and I had time to get acquainted before rehearsals but we didn't have much in common. I asked him about his hobbies, Justin likes motorcycles, and exotic pets, which I know nothing about. I love basketball and Justin doesn't watch sports. However, because of the news cycle reporting the police killing of Michael Brown (Micheal Brown was an unarmed 18 year old Black man murdered by a Ferguson Missouri police officer) I asked Justin, how do the police treat blacks in Nashville? And, boom we connected. Justin grew up in a black neighborhood, just as I did. We both shared our child and adulthood experiences with state crime. It was unnerving to realize that even though we were strangers, living in separate states, with uncommon interest, we shared a bond over something we feared and hated, police brutality. I learned through this experience and many others that state crime isn't a Chicago problem, or an inner-city problem, it's world-wide and systematic.

References

Levin, Mike (1997) *How to be a Working Musician; A Practical Guide to Earning Money in the Music Business.* New York, NY, Billboard Books

Thompson Amir "QuestLove" & Greenman Ben (2013) *Mo Meta Blues; The World According to Questlove* New York, NY Grand Central Publishing Hachette Book Group

E. Sheila, Holden Wendy (2015) *The Beat of My Own Drum* New York, NY Atria Paperback an Imprint of Simon and Schuster, Inc.

Guy Buddy, Ritz Donald (2012) *When I Left Home* Philadelphia P.A.; Da Capo Press

Harper Hill (2011) *The Wealth Cure; Putting Money in its Place* New York, NY Gotham Books a member of Penguin Group

Green, Robert (2012) New York, New York Penguin Books

Benelli Mark, (2016) *Screamin' Jay Hawkins All-Time Greatest Hits* New York, NY Metropolitan Books Henry Holt Company